VISUAL QUICKSTART GUIDE

Windows 98

Steve Sagman

◯ **Peachpit Press**

Visual QuickStart Guide
Windows 98
Steve Sagman

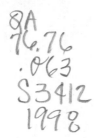

Peachpit Press
1249 Eighth Street
Berkeley, CA 94710
(510) 524-2178
(510) 524-2221 (fax)

Find us on the World Wide Web at: http://www.peachpit.com

Peachpit Press is a division of Addison Wesley Longman

Copyright © 1998 by Steve Sagman

Cover design: The Visual Group

Trademarks

Microsoft and Microsoft Windows are registered trademarks of Microsoft Corporation.

ISBN: 0-201-69689-4

0 9 8 7 6 5 4 3 2 1

Printed in the United States.

Printed on recycled paper

Thank You

To **Corbin Collins, Kate Reber, Cheryl Applewood,** and **Nancy Ruenzel** at Peachpit Press.

To **Rick Altman** and **Rebecca Bridges Altman** for contributing Chapters 2 and 6 to the previous edition.

To **Eric** and **Lola** for their patience and love.

Dedication

To Rich Delaney and Joe Lanzilotta, great friends I respect and admire for their spirit and strength.

About the Author

More than a million readers worldwide know Steve Sagman's books on PC software, including his international best-sellers on Harvard Graphics and PowerPoint. In 1995, his book *Traveling The Microsoft Network* was given the Award of Achievement for Design from the Society of Technical Communication.

His company, Studioserv (www.studioserv.com), provides book packaging and development, courseware, user documentation, and user interface consulting.

He welcomes comments, questions, and suggestions and can be reached at steves@studioserv.com.

Other Books by Steve Sagman

The Official Microsoft Image Composer Book

Running PowerPoint 97

*Windows 95: Visual QuickStart Guide***

Running PowerPoint for Windows 95

Traveling The Microsoft Network

*Running Windows 95**

Microsoft Office for Macintosh: Visual QuickStart Guide

*Microsoft Office for Windows: Visual QuickStart Guide***

*Harvard Graphics for Windows 2: Visual QuickStart Guide***

Running PowerPoint 4

The PC Bible ***

Mastering CorelDraw 4 ***

*Using 1-2-3 for Windows Release 4**

Using Freelance Graphics 2

Mastering CorelDraw 3 ***

Using Windows Draw

*Getting Your Start in Hollywood***

1-2-3 Graphics Techniques

Using Harvard Graphics

* Contributor.

** Also published by Peachpit Press.

Table of Contents

Part 1 Introducing Windows 98

1. Windows Basics

2. Using the Accessories

3. Disks, Folders, and Files

Part 2 Managing Your Computer

7. Maintaining Your Computer

8. Adding Hardware and Software

Part 3 Going Online

9. Setting Up a Connection

10. Exchanging E-Mail

Table of Contents

11. Browsing the Internet

Part 4 Portable and Workgroup Computing

12. Portable Computing

13. **Connecting to a Network**

Table of Contents

Part 1
Introducing
Windows 98

Part 1
Introducing
Windows 98

Windows Basics

In this Chapter...

You will learn the fundamental and vital things that you really must understand to be productive with Windows 98. You'll learn to understand the basic Windows desktop, for example, and how to perform everyday tasks like starting programs, using menus, and switching between windows on the screen.

Even if you think you know the basics, you might still find time-saving gems in the chapter's dozens of tips. Somehow there's always a better and faster way to do it in Windows. One less step, or a couple of clicks fewer can add up to real time savings over the long run.

In this Chapter

What Is Windows?

Windows puts a graphical working environment on a PC's screen so you can operate your computer with visual controls rather than typed commands. It gives you icons, menus, and buttons that you can click with the mouse to do things like organize your folders and files, run programs, control your printer, and go online with your modem and browse the Internet.

Basically, Windows does two things: it lets you manage your computer (the hardware and software in your system), and it runs programs.

Managing your computer means tasks like installing a new printer or setting up an Internet connection. It also includes such activities as deleting old files, backing up your collection of documents to diskettes for safe-keeping, or moving all the files for a project into their own folder.

Running programs means starting your favorite word processor, Web browser, or even game. It also means giving you the power to open a second program in a separate window and then switch back and forth between programs, so you can do chores like check your e-mail in an e-mail program while leaving your word processor open in its own window.

Windows offers several key advantages over the way PCs used to work with DOS. Before Windows, every program had its own unique screens and commands to learn and remember. Now Windows programs, even those from different companies, look alike and work similarly. Once you've learned basic skills in one program, you can

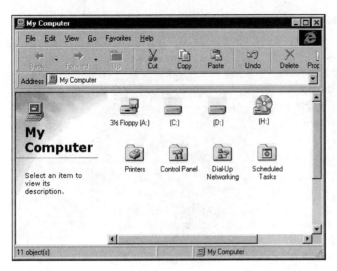

transfer your knowledge to other programs easily. For example, after you've learned that the Save command is always on the File menu, you'll be able to save your work in any Windows program.

Windows also provides a set of basic features that all your programs can use. For example, new fonts that you install in Windows are available to every Windows program. The new font shows up in your word processor, spreadsheet, graphics program, and others. Similarly, when you install a printer in a Windows, every program can print to it. Windows also provides a mechanism that lets you transfer information from one program to another without having to go through elaborate importing and exporting procedures. Anything you "copy" in a program goes to the Windows Clipboard. When you switch to another program and then "paste," the contents of the Clipboard appear in the second program. This gives you the ability to quickly and easily move things like passages of text from one program to another. For example, you can compose a letter in a word processor and then copy and paste it into an e-mail message.

If You're Upgrading from Windows 95

Windows 98 offers a number of evolutionary changes to the basic capabilities of Windows 95. Some are new features, and some are features that you could install into Windows 95, but that are now fully integrated. Here are some of the key improvements:

Integrated Internet Explorer

Microsoft's Web browser is now built in to Windows 98. You can use Internet Explorer to view Web pages on the Internet, Web pages on your company's internal intranet, or Web pages on your own disk drives. **(Figure 1)**

Outlook Express

An integral part of Internet Explorer is its e-mail program, Outlook Express, which lets you send and receive Internet e-mail messages and browse Internet news discussion boards. **(Figure 2)**

Windows Update

Registered Windows 98 users can use the Update Manager and their modem to automatically connect to the Microsoft Web site and access the latest drivers and operating system files. The Update Manager scans your system and updates outdated components. **(Figure 3)**

Figure 1. *Internet Explorer.*

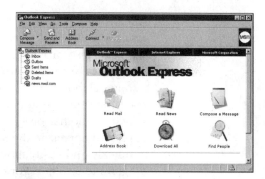

Figure 2. *Outlook Express.*

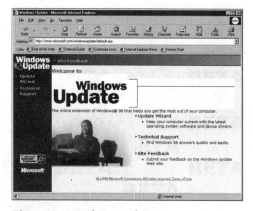

Figure 3. *Windows Update.*

Figure 4. *Internet Connection Wizard.*

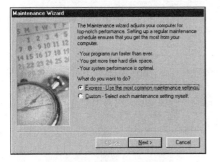

Figure 5. *Maintenance Wizard.*

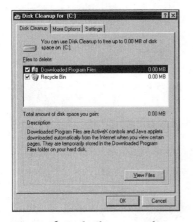

Figure 6. *Disk Cleanup utility.*

Internet Connection Wizard

The Internet Connection Wizard helps you set up your Internet connection the first time. It offers a list of Internet Service Providers with which you can set up an account, and then it sets up your connection automatically. **(Figure 4)**

Windows Maintenance Wizard

The Windows Maintenance Wizard can schedule regular tune-up jobs automatically. They can happen overnight, for example, while you sleep. The wizard can optimize your hard disk, delete unnecessary files, and even set up your programs so they launch faster. **(Figure 5)**

Disk Cleanup

Disk Cleanup automates the job of removing unnecessary files from your hard disk. **(Figure 6)**

Support for Windows TV

If your system has a TV tuner board installed, Windows 98 allows you to use your PC to receive and display TV shows. The Windows 98 Program Guide, updated continuously, lists current shows and lets you switch to them instantly.

If You're Upgrading from Windows 95

Display Enhancements

The dialog box you use to change your system's video settings is enhanced, and several formerly optional capabilities are now integrated, such as font smoothing, which improves the appearance of on-screen text, and full window drag, which allows you to see the contents of windows as you move them. **(Figure 7)**

Multilink Connections

With Windows 98, you can use two modems or two ISDN channels to double the speed of your connection. **(Figure 8)**

Remote Access Server

With Windows 98, you can set up your system to answer modem calls while you are away from your machine. Those who have the proper password can connect to your machine with a modem and transfer files and print as if they were directly connected through a network. **(Figure 9)**

Behind-the-Scenes Technical Improvements

Many of the improvements in Windows 98 are not immediately evident, but they're helpful when you want to take advantage of the latest hardware and software advances. Windows 98 supports FAT32, a file system that lets your disks store files much more efficiently to save space. It also provides the newest power management capabilities and PC card support for portable computing. In addition, Windows 98 supports Universal Serial Bus (USB) Accelerated Graphics Port (AGP), Digital Video Disc (DVD), and Infrared file transfers (IrDA).

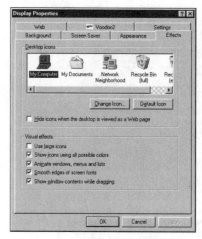

Figure 7. *Display properties.*

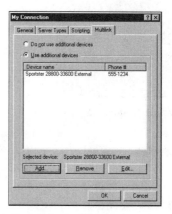

Figure 8. *Multilink tab.*

Figure 9. *Dial-Up Server dialog box.*

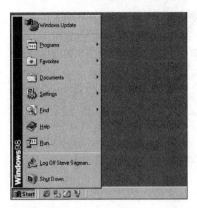

Figure 10. *Start menu.*

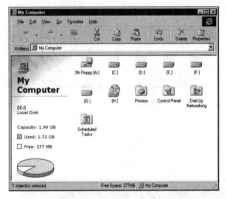

Figure 11. *My Computer window.*

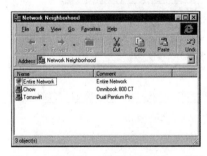

Figure 12. *Network Neighborhood window.*

If You're Upgrading from Windows 3.1

Windows 98 is a substantial change from earlier versions of Windows (Windows 3.1 and Windows for Workgroups 3.11). It offers not only a totally revamped screen appearance, but hundreds of significant changes to the way you work and new capabilities that can ease your everyday use of the computer.

Here are some of the new features:

Start menu

The Start button, always visible at the lower left corner of the screen, opens a pop-up Start menu that lists all your installed programs. **(Figure 10)**

My Computer

Double-clicking the My Computer icon on the main Windows screen opens a window that shows your system's disks and other resources. **(Figure 11)**

Network Neighborhood

If you are connected to a network, double-clicking this button lets you browse the network's folders, files, and printers. **(Figure 12)**

Taskbar

Like the Start button, the Taskbar is always at the bottom of the screen. Every window you open puts another button on the taskbar. You can click the buttons to switch among windows. **(Figure 13)**

Figure 13. *Taskbar.*

Recycle Bin

Files that you delete are sent to the Recycle Bin so you can retrieve them, until you empty the bin. **(Figure 14)**

Find command

The Find command on the Start menu lets you easily find any folder or file on your disk or on any computer on your network. **(Figure 15)**

Explorer

This replacement to the Windows File Manager lets you view and manage the folders and files on your disks. **(Figure 16)**

Long filenames

Filenames can now be 256 characters long, not just the 8 characters (plus a three-character extension) of DOS. **(Figure 17)**

Figure 14. *The Recycle Bin.*

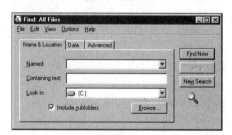

Figure 15. *Find dialog box.*

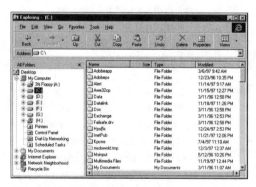

Figure 16. *Windows Explorer.*

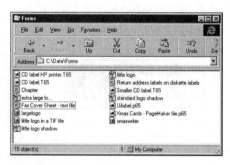

Figure 17. *Long filenames.*

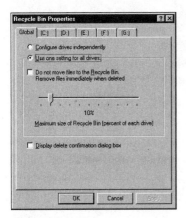

Figure 18. *Properties for the Recycle Bin.*

Figure 19. *Documents list.*

Figure 20. *Previewing an image.*

Properties

Nearly everything in Windows has settings called properties. You can right click something and then inspect or adjust its properties. **(Figure 18)**

Documents list

From the Start menu, you can see a list of the files you have opened recently and reopen them quickly. **(Figure 19)**

File previews

In Web Page view, a preview shows the contents of the file that you have selected. **(Figure 20)**

Wizards

Special step-by-step guides called Wizards lead you through many common procedures, such as sending a fax or adding new hardware. **(Figure 21)**

Figure 21. *A wizard.*

If You're Upgrading from Windows 3.1

Desktop shortcuts

Icons that start programs are called shortcuts. They can be placed right on the desktop or organized into folders on the desktop. **(Figure 22)**

Figure 22. *A shortcut.*

Easy font viewing and installation

The Font folder in the Windows Control Panel holds all the TrueType fonts installed on your system, and it gives you the tools to easily view, delete, and install fonts. **(Figure 23)**

File synchronization for portable computers

The Briefcase can synchronize files on your laptop with those on your desktop computer, so you'll always have the latest updates in both places. **(Figure 24)**

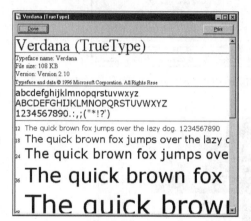

Figure 23. *Viewing a font.*

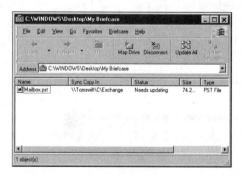

Figure 24. *The Briefcase.*

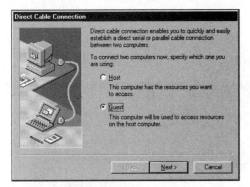

Figure 25. *Direct Cable Connection wizard.*

Figure 26. *Dial-Up Networking connectoids.*

Direct Cable Connection

When you connect a laptop to another computer with a cable, you can use Direct Cable Connection to easily transfer files between the two computers. **(Figure 25)**

Docking detection

Windows can detect when you've docked a portable computer to a docking station and automatically switch to the hardware profile that contains support for the devices in the dock.

Dial-Up Networking

When you are traveling, you can use Dial-Up Networking to call into your computer by modem and work with the files on it as though you were still connected. **(Figure 26)**

If You're Upgrading from Windows 3.1

The Windows Desktop

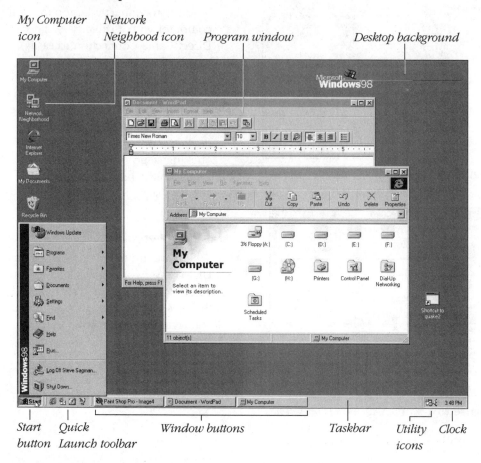

My Computer icon   Network Neighbood icon   Program window   Desktop background

Start button   Quick Launch toolbar   Window buttons   Taskbar   Utility icons   Clock

Figure 27. *The Windows 98 Desktop.*

My Computer icon

Double-click the My Computer icon to open the My Computer window, which shows the resources available in your computer. If a desktop icon like "My Computer" is underlined, you may be able to single-click it.

Network Neighborhood icon

Double-click the Network Neighborhood icon to view the other computers that are available on your office network.

Program window

A program window displays a program that you've started. More than one program can run at a time, each in its own window.

Desktop background

The Windows background, the "desktop," occupies the entire screen. You can change its display properties, including its color, by right-clicking anywhere on the desktop.

Start button

Click this button to open the Start menu, which lets you view a clickable list of the programs you can run on your system. It also lets you choose a document that you have used recently, change your system's settings, find a file, get help, or run a DOS program. Strangely, you must also click the Start button to stop, or shut down, your computer.

Quick Launch toolbar

Click the icons on the Quick Launch toolbar on the Taskbar to start certain programs that you can start instantly. You can add your own icons here to make starting your favorite programs easy.

Window buttons

Each program window has a corresponding window button on the Taskbar. Click the button to open that program window on top of all other windows. Click the button again to "minimize" the window, temporarily closing it but leaving its program running.

Taskbar

The Taskbar contains the Start button, the window buttons, and a panel at the right, which holds the clock and icons for utility programs that you can run, such as the volume control.

Utility icons

Handy programs that perform minor functions are often available as utility icons on the taskbar. Double-click these icons to run their utilities. Some utility icons give you options when you right-click them.

Clock

The current time. Place the mouse pointer on the clock without clicking to see the date. Double-click the clock to set the time zone and the current time.

The Windows Desktop

A Typical Window

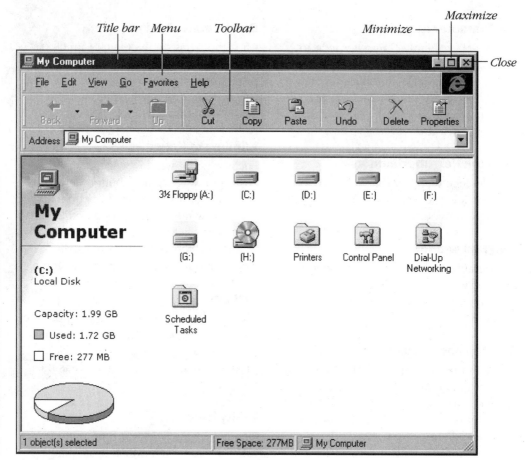

Figure 28. *A typical window.*

Title bar

Identifies the window name.

Menu

Holds a horizontal list of commands you can click.

Toolbar

Contains buttons for the commands you use most often.

Minimize

Reduces the window to a button on the taskbar. Click the taskbar button to reopen the window.

Maximize

Expands a window to fill the screen.

Close

Closes a window. Shuts down a program in a program window.

Figure 28. *The lower-left window is active. The other window is inactive.*

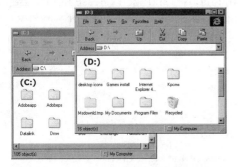

Figure 29. *The upper-right window is active. The other window is inactive.*

Activating Windows

Although you can simultaneously open a number of windows on the Windows desktop, you can work in only one window at a time. The other windows continue to run their programs, but only one window can be "active."

The active window is identifiable by its vivid title bar. The title bars of all the other windows are dimmed. **(Figures 28–29)**

Click anywhere in a window to make it active.

or

Click the window button for the window on the Taskbar.

✔ Tip

■ You can also press Alt+Esc to switch to the next open window.

Using the Mouse

Moving the mouse on the desktop moves the pointer on the screen. Rolling the ball on a trackball or moving your finger across a trackpad also moves the mouse pointer. Here are the three basic mouse techniques:

Click

Place the pointer on something and click the left mouse button once.

Double-click

Place the pointer on something and then click the left mouse button twice quickly without moving the mouse. Double-click a disk or folder to show its contents, double-click an icon to start a program, or double-click a word to select it.

Drag

Place the pointer on something, press and hold down the mouse button, move the mouse, and then release the mouse button. Drag to highlight text or move an object or window.

Terminology

Select

Click an object on the screen or drag across text. Your next action will affect what you've selected.

Press

Press a key on the keyboard.

Drop-down list

Click the drop-down arrow at the right end of a text box to pull down a list of alternatives, then click an item on the list.

Check/ Uncheck

Click the check box next to an option to turn it on or off. A checked box indicates that the option is turned on.

Scroll

Use the scroll bar to the right of a list or window to move up or down through the list or window. Drag the scroll button along the scroll bar or click the up or down arrow buttons at the ends of the scroll bar. You can also click in between the buttons to scroll a screenful at a time.

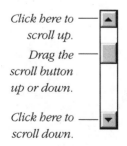

Click here to scroll up.

Drag the scroll button up or down.

Click here to scroll down.

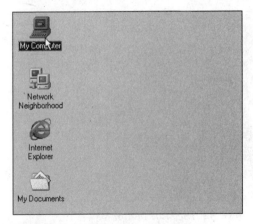

Figure 30. *Double-click an icon.*

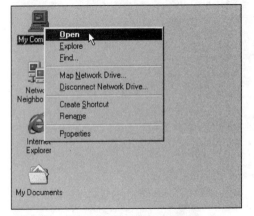

Figure 31. *The shortcut menu appears when you right-click an icon.*

Starting Programs by Clicking Icons on the Desktop

Some programs that come with Windows, such as Internet Explorer or the Recycle Bin, appear as icons on the Windows desktop. You can create additional icons on the desktop for programs you use often by creating shortcuts.

1. Double-click a program's icon.
(Figure 30)

or

1. Click the icon with the right mouse button.

2. From the shortcut menu, choose Open.
(Figure 31)

✔ Tip

■ To learn more about a program represented by an icon, right-click the icon, and then choose Properties on the shortcut menu.

Starting Programs by Clicking Icons

Starting Programs from the Start Menu

The programs you have installed in Windows are available on the Start menu.

1. Click the Start button at the left end of the Taskbar. **(Figure 32)**
2. Move the mouse pointer up to the word "Programs." **(Figure 33)**
3. When the Programs submenu pops out **(Figure 34)**, move the pointer to the program or program group that you want and then click.

✔ Tips

■ Program groups on the Programs submenu lead to further submenus. A right arrow appears next to these items.

■ When you install programs, they are almost always added to the Start menu automatically.

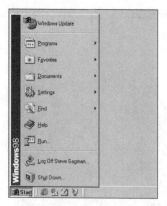

Figure 32. *The Start button.*

Figure 33. *Move the pointer to "Programs."*

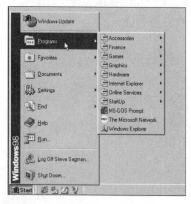

Figure 34. *Choose a program or one of the program groups from the Programs submenu.*

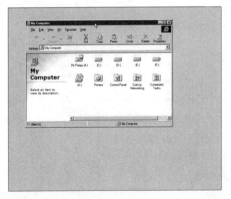

Figure 35. *Place the pointer on the title bar.*

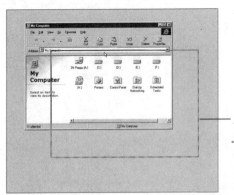

Figure 36. *Hold down the mouse button and move the mouse.*

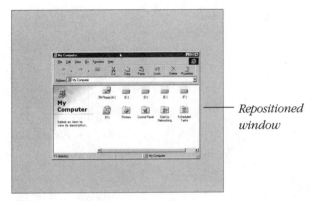

Figure 37. *Release the mouse button.*

Moving Windows

1. Place the mouse pointer on the window's title bar. **(Figure 35)**

2. Hold down the mouse button.

3. Move the mouse to move the window. **(Figure 36)**

4. Release the mouse button when the window is correctly placed. **(Figure 37)**

✔ Tip

■ If "Show window contents while dragging" is turned on, the whole window and its contents, not just the gray window frame, will move around the screen.

Drag the window frame into position and release the mouse button.

Repositioned window

Moving Windows

Sizing Windows

1. Position the mouse pointer on the edge of a window. **(Figure 38)**

2. Press and hold down the mouse button and move the mouse to drag the edge of the window. **(Figure 39)**

3. Release the mouse button. **(Figure 40)**

✔ Tip

■ Many windows in Windows 98 have a ridged tab at the lower right corner that you can drag to resize the window. **(Figure 41)**

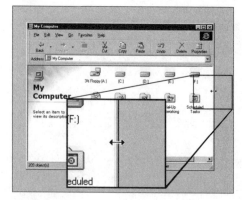

Figure 38. *Place the mouse pointer on a window's edge.*

Figure 39. *Hold down the mouse button and drag the edge.*

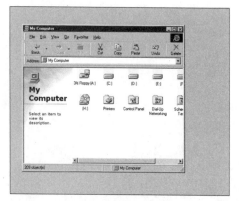

Figure 40. *Release the mouse button.*

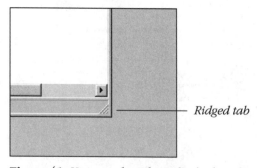

Figure 41. *You can drag this ridged tab at the corner to resize a window.*

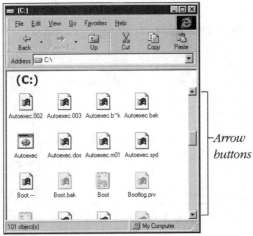

Figure 42. *Click an arrow button.*

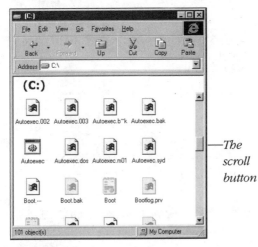

Figure 43. *Drag the scroll button.*

Figure 44. *Click on the scroll bar.*

Scrolling the Contents of Windows

When a window contains more information than can fit on one screen, scroll bars appear along the bottom or along the right edge of the window. Use these scroll bars to reposition the contents within the window.

Click on one of the arrow buttons at the ends of a scroll bar. **(Figure 42)**

or

Drag the scroll button along the scroll bar. **(Figure 43)**

or

Click along the length of the scroll bar to jump the window to that point. **(Figure 44)**

—*Arrow buttons*

—*The scroll button*

— *Click within the scroll bar.*

Closing Windows

Click the Close button at the upper right corner of the window.
(Figure 45)

or

Right-click the title bar and choose Close from the shortcut menu.
(Figure 46)

or

Click the application icon at the left end of the title bar and choose Close from the control menu. **(Figure 47)**

or

Double-click the application icon at the left end of the title bar.

or

Press Alt+F4.

The Close button

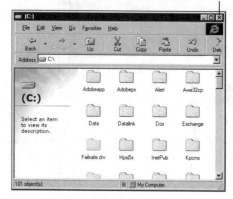

Figure 45. *Click the close button.*

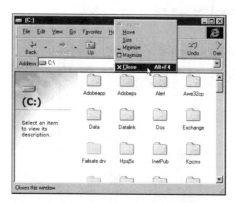

Figure 46. *Right-click the title bar.*

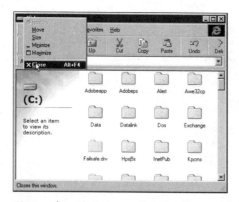

Figure 47. *Click the application icon and choose Close from the control menu.*

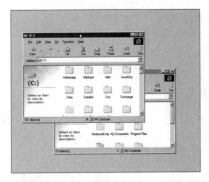

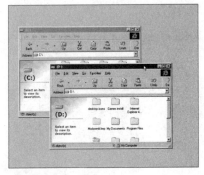

Switching Between Windows

Click any visible part of a window to bring it to the front. **(Figure 48)**

or

Click the button for the window on the Taskbar. **(Figure 49)**

or

Press Alt+Tab until the icon for the window is selected and then release both keys. **(Figure 50)**

or

Press Alt+Esc to move to the next window on the desktop.

Figure 48. *Click a window to bring it to the front.*

Window buttons

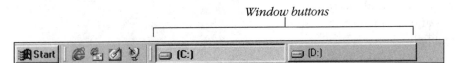

Figure 49. *Click a button on the Taskbar.*

Figure 50. *Press Alt+Tab repeatedly until the icon is selected for the program that you want.*

Using Menus

Every application has a horizontal menu bar that crosses the top of the window. Each menu name on the menu bar represents a group of commands or options on a vertical menu.

1. Click a menu name to open a vertical menu. **(Figure 51)**

or

Press Alt and then press the underlined letter in the menu name.

2. Click a command or option on a vertical menu. **(Figure 52)**

or

Press the underlined letter in a command or option.

✔ Tips

■ After you open a menu, you can press the right and left arrow keys to open adjacent menus on the menu bar.

■ To close a menu, click the menu name again or press Esc until the menu disappears and the menu name is no longer highlighted.

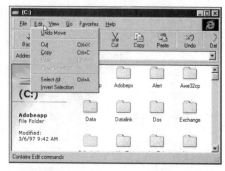

Figure 51. *Click a menu name.*

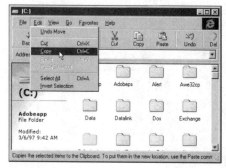

Figure 52. *Click a menu command.*

Selecting Options in Dialog Boxes

Click a dialog box **tab** *to bring a different set of options to the front.*

*Press **Tab** on the keyboard to move to the **next entry**. Press **Shift+Tab** to move to the **previous** entry.*

*Click a **check box** to turn an option on or off. An "x" in a check box means the option is turned on.*

*Some dialog boxes show a **preview** of changes you are about to make.*

*Click **OK** after you change settings or press **Enter**. Click **Cancel** to abandon changes you've made or press **Esc**.*

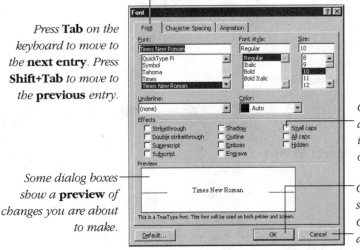

Figure 53. *A typical dialog box.*

*Click the **Help** button and then click a setting to get help about that setting.*

Double-click an entry in a text box to select it. Then you can type a replacement.

Round buttons *provide an either/or choice. Only one choice can be turned on.*

*Click a **drop-down menu button** to see a list of alternatives for an option.*

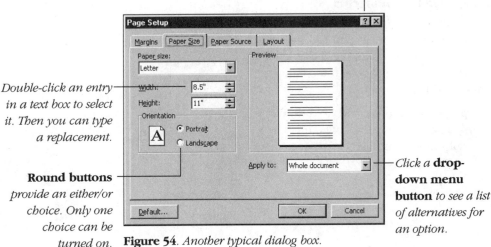

Figure 54. *Another typical dialog box.*

Using Shortcut Menus

Almost everything on the Windows desktop has a shortcut menu that you can open by right-clicking the item. The shortcut menu provides specific commands or options for that item. Even the desktop itself has a shortcut menu you can use to change the appearance of the desktop. The shortcut menus for most items includes "Properties," an option you can click to inspect and modify the object's settings.

1. Click any item on the desktop with the right mouse button. **(Figures 55–56)**

✔ Tips

■ To close a shortcut menu, click anywhere else on the desktop.

■ As you learn Windows 98, don't be afraid to right-click just about anything you see. You'll probably find a shortcut menu.

Using Keyboard Shortcuts

The underlined letter in a menu command is the keyboard shortcut you can press. When the menu is open, press this letter on the keyboard to choose the command. **(Figure 57)**

To open a menu, press and hold down the Alt key and press the keyboard shortcut in the menu name.

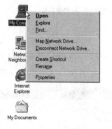

Figure 55. *The shortcut menu for My Computer.*

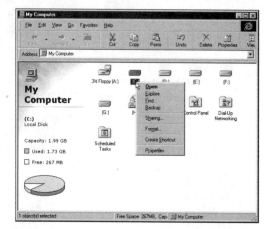

Figure 56. *The shortcut menu for a disk icon.*

Figure 57. *A menu.*

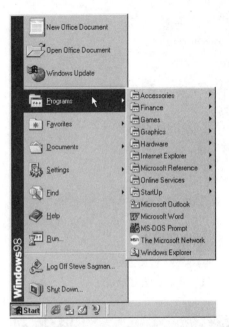

Figure 58. *Choose Programs from the Start menu.*

Starting an MS-DOS Window

To run a favorite DOS program, you can open an MS-DOS window. Inside the window, you can work just as you would in DOS if Windows was not installed. To change advanced settings for the DOS window, right-click the title bar and then choose Properties from the shortcut menu.

1. Click the Start button.
2. Choose Programs. **(Figure 58)**
3. On the Programs submenu, click MS-DOS Prompt. **(Figure 59)**

✔ Tips

■ When you resize the DOS window, the text inside resizes also.

■ To expand the DOS window so it fills the screen, click the Expand button on the toolbar.

■ To restore an expanded window, press Alt+Enter.

■ When you finish working in a DOS window, type "Exit" at the DOS prompt, or close the DOS window as you would any other window.

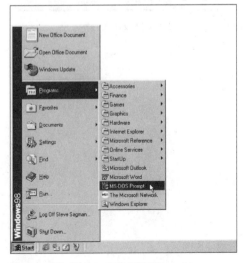

Figure 59. *Choose MS-DOS Prompt.*

Expand button

Figure 60. *An MS-DOS window.*

Shutting Down the Computer

Before you turn off the computer, always remember to shut down Windows. This saves the state of Windows so it will restart the next time with all the same changes. It also ensures that you do not have any unsaved files in applications. If you simply turn off the computer, you may run the risk of damaging these files.

1. Click the Start menu.
2. Choose Shut Down. **(Figure 61)**
3. On the Shut Down Windows dialog box, choose one of the three options, described below
4. Click OK or press Enter. **(Figure 62)**

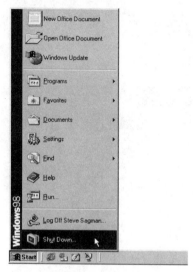

Figure 61. *Choose Shut Down.*

Shut Down Options

Shut down checks to be sure that no unsaved files remain in applications, saves the state of Windows, and then displays a "You May Now Safely Turn Off the Computer" screen.

Restart shuts down Windows and then reboots your machine as though you'd turned it off and then back on.

Restart in MS-DOS mode shuts down the computer and then reboots the computer and loads MS-DOS. When the computer restarts you will see a standard DOS prompt. When you finish working in DOS, type "Exit" at the DOS prompt to return to Windows.

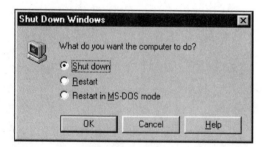

Figure 62. *The Shut Down options.*

Using the Accessories

In this Chapter...

In this Chapter...

You will learn about the accessories that come with Windows 98. The accessories are little programs that perform useful functions quickly and easily. WordPad is a simple word processing program, for example, that lets you type short notes and edit simple documents. It offers only a fraction of the functionality of a major word processing program, such as Microsoft Word.

This chapter will cover the accessories you'll probably use most often: WordPad, Notepad, Paint, Calculator, Phone Dialer, and the CD Player.

Opening an Accessory

The accessories are listed on the Accessories menu. To display this menu, follow these steps:

1. Click the Start button. **(Figure 1)**
2. From the Start menu, choose Programs.
3. From the Programs submenu, choose Accessories. **(Figure 2)**
4. From the Accessories submenu, choose the accessory you want to use, such as WordPad.

Figure 1. *Click the Start button.*

Figure 2. *Choose Accessories from the Programs submenu.*

Opening an Accessory

Figure 3. *Choose WordPad from the Accessories submenu.*

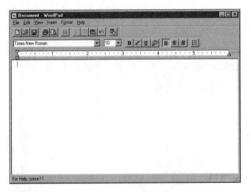

Figure 4. *A new WordPad document.*

Figure 5. *The WordPad View menu.*

Typing Documents in WordPad

Although it won't replace a full word processing program, such as Microsoft Word, WordPad is a no-frills text editor that is similar to the Write program that came with earlier versions of Windows. It does a fine job with short text files.

1. Open the WordPad accessory.
(Figure 3)

2. In the new document that is automatically displayed, begin typing.
(Figure 4)

✔ Tips

■ If you use WordPad frequently, you can create a shortcut to it on your desktop.

■ If you do not see the toolbar, format bar, or the ruler, choose them from the View menu to display them.
(Figure 5)

Editing a Document in WordPad

1. Click in the text to place the insertion point at the spot that needs editing.

2. To delete text to the right of the insertion point, press the Delete key. To delete text to the left, press the Backspace key.

3. To insert text at the insertion point, just begin typing.

Typing/Editing Documents in WordPad

Moving Text in WordPad

1. Select the text to be moved.
(Figure 6)

2. Click the Cut button on the toolbar.
(Figure 7)

3. Click to place the mouse pointer where you want the text to appear.
(Figure 8)

4. Click the Paste button on the toolbar.
(Figure 9)

✔ Tips

■ If you accidentally delete text, you can recover it by clicking the Undo button on the toolbar. **(Figure 9)**

■ Another way to move text is to select the text and then drag it to a new location.

■ To replace text, you can select the unwanted text and then type the new text in its place.

Selected text

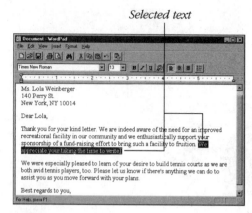

Figure 6. *Select the text.*

Cut button

Figure 7. *Click the Cut button.*

Click to place the mouse pointer.

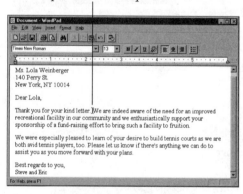

Figure 8. *Click to place the mouse pointer where you want the text to appear.*

Paste button   Undo button

Figure 9. *Click the Paste button.*

Moving Text in WordPad

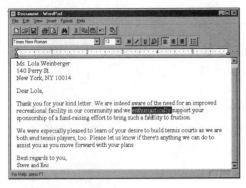

Figure 10. *Select the text to format.*

Figure 11. *The format toolbar.*

Figure 12. *The Font Size field.*

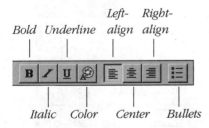

Figure 13. *The Format bar.*

Formatting Text in WordPad

1. Select the text that you want to format. **(Figure 10)**

2. To change the font, click the Font field on the format bar, and choose a different font from the drop-down list. **(Figure 11)**

3. To change the type size, click the Font Size field on the format bar. **(Figure 12)**

4. To change other formatting, click a formatting button on the Format bar. **(Figure 13)**

✔ Tips

■ **Figure 14** shows some of the formatting choices you can make.

■ The Format menu offers additional formatting options. **(Figure 15)**

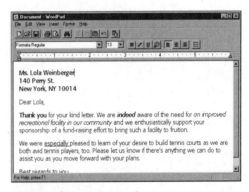

Figure 14. *Sample text formatting.*

Figure 15. *The Format menu.*

Saving a Document in WordPad

1. From the File menu, choose Save As.

   or

   Click the Save button on the toolbar. **(Figure 16)**

2. Choose a folder in which to place the new file. **(Figure 17–18)**

3. In the File name field, type a descriptive name. **(Figure 19)**

4. Click the Save button. **(Figure 19)**

✔ Tip

■ To resave a file, click the Save button again.

Save button

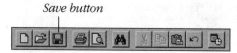

Figure 16. *The toolbar.*

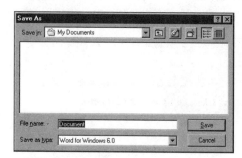

Figure 17. *The Save As dialog box.*

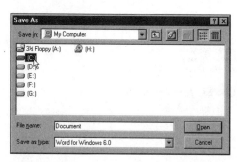

Figure 18. *Navigate to the disk and folder for the file.*

Click Save

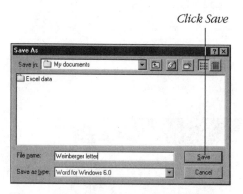

Figure 19. *Enter a file name and click Save.*

Figure 20. *The Print dialog box.*

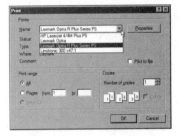

Figure 21. *Choose a printer from the name drop-down list.*

Print button   *Print Preview button*

Figure 22. *Click the Print button*

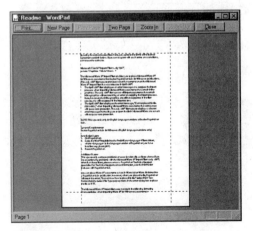

Figure 23. *The Print Preview.*

Printing in WordPad

1. From the File menu, choose Print. The Print dialog box appears. **(Figure 20)**

2. If you have more than one printer, confirm that the correct printer is selected in the Name field. If it's not, click the down-arrow button and choose the printer you want from the Name pull-down list. **(Figure 21)**

3. Click OK.

✔ Tips

- If you are sure the correct printer is selected, or if you have only one printer, you can print the document by simply clicking the Print button on the toolbar. **(Figure 22)** This button prints the entire document without displaying the Print dialog box.

- To see a full-page preview of your document before printing it **(Figure 23)**, choose Print Preview from the File menu or click the Print Preview button on the toolbar. **(Figure 22)**

Printing in WordPad

Using Notepad

Notepad, Windows 98's ultra-simple text editor, is useful for editing basic system files (such as AUTOEXEC.BAT and CONFIG.SYS), and other text-only files (such as README.TXT files). Notepad offers no text formatting, however.

Most often, you'll be using Notepad to open and edit existing text files. **(Figure 24)**

1. Open the Notepad accessory.

2. From the File menu in Notepad, choose Open.

3. Navigate to the drive and folder where the text file is located. **(Figures 25–26)**

4. Click the name of the file and then click Open. **(Figure 27)**

    or

    Double-click the file name.

5. Make the corrections you want.

6. To save the file with the same name, choose Save from the File menu.

✔ Tip

■ If you see a text file in My Computer or The Explorer and you want to open it in Notepad, just double-click the Notepad icon that's above the file name. **(Figure 28)**

Figure 24. *The Notepad window.*

Figure 25. *Navigate to the folder and file you want.*

Figure 26. *Click a drive letter to see its contents.*

Figure 27. *Select a file and click Open.*

Figure 28. *Notepad icon.*

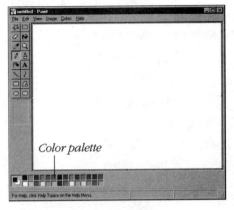

Figure 29. *The Paint window.*

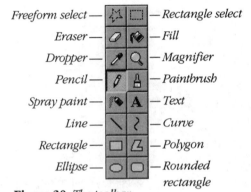

Freeform select — Rectangle select
Eraser — Fill
Dropper — Magnifier
Pencil — Paintbrush
Spray paint — Text
Line — Curve
Rectangle — Polygon
Ellipse — Rounded rectangle

Figure 30. *The toolbar.*

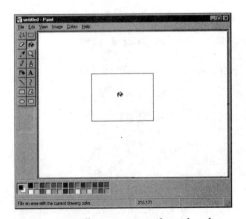

Figure 31. *Filling a rectangle with color.*

Painting with Paint

Using Microsoft Paint, you can create bitmap color paintings with basic shapes, such as circles, rectangles, and lines. You can also edit existing pictures that are in the BMP (short for "bitmap") file format.

To work with pictures, such as those you scan or take with a digital camera, you will want to use a more powerful picture editing program, such as PaintShop Pro, which is available for downloading on the Internet.

1. Open the Paint accessory. An empty page is automatically displayed. **(Figure 29)**

2. Before painting an object, click the color you want on the color palette. **(Figure 29)**

3. To create objects, click a tool, place the mouse pointer, hold down the mouse button, and move the mouse. **(Figure 30)**

4. To fill an object with color, choose the Fill tool, click a color on the color palette, and then click inside the object to be filled. **(Figure 31)**

✔ **Tip**

■ If you get unexpected results when drawing or filling objects, choose Undo from the Edit menu.

Painting with Paint

Zooming In on a Picture

While modifying a painting, you may need to zoom in so you can see more detail.

1. Click the Magnifier button on the toolbox. **(Figure 32)**
2. Click the image at the spot you'd like to zoom in on. **(Figure 33)**

✔ Tip

■ You can open a Thumbnail window to see the overall view while you are zoomed in. From the View menu, choose Zoom, and then choose Show Thumbnail from the Zoom submenu. **(Figure 34)**

Magnifier button

Figure 32. *Click the Magnifier button on the toolbox.*

Figure 33. *Click at the spot to zoom in on.*

Thumbnail window

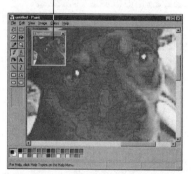

Figure 34. *The Thumbnail window shows an unmagnified view.*

Zooming In on a Picture

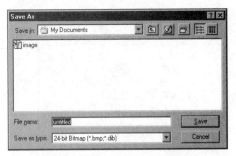

Figure 35. *The Save As dialog box.*

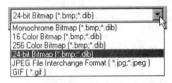

Figure 36. *Choose a graphics file format.*

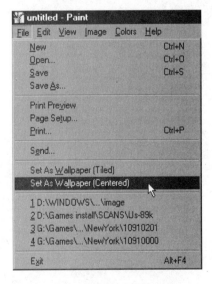

Figure 37. *Setting an image as the Windows desktop wallpaper.*

Saving a Painting

1. From the File menu, choose Save As. The Save As dialog box appears. **(Figure 35)**

2. In the File name field, type a descriptive name. Paint will automatically add a .BMP extension.

3. From the Save as Type drop-down list, choose a graphics file format. **(Figure 36)**

4. Choose a location for the new file.

5. Click the Save button.

✔ Tips

■ For more realism and color accuracy, save the file in the 256 Color or 24-bit Color file format. Bear in mind, though, that these formats create much bigger files, so don't choose them unless you really need them. You may want to experiment with the different formats to see which one produces the smallest file, yet still gives you the desired results.

■ The Save as Wallpaper options on the File menu place a copy of the current painting on your Windows desktop background. **(Figure 37)** "Tiled" repeats the image to fill the background, like mosaic tiles. "Centered" places a single copy of the image at the middle of the the background.

Saving a Painting

Calculating with the Calculator

Use the Calculator accessory to perform quick mathematical operations, and then, if you like, paste the result into another application.

1. Open the Calculator accessory. The Calculator window appears. **(Figure 38)**

2. Enter numbers using the keyboard or by clicking the onscreen number keys with the mouse.

3. Press Enter or click the equal sign (=) in Calculator to display the result of your calculation.

✔ Tips

- If you make a typing mistake, press Backspace or click the Backspace button in Calculator.

- To clear the number in Calculator's display, click the CE button. To clear the current calculation, click the C button.

Pasting a Result Into Another Program

1. From Calculator's Edit menu, choose Copy. **(Figure 39)**

2. Switch to the other program and position the insertion point where you want the result to appear.

3. From the program's Edit menu, choose Paste.

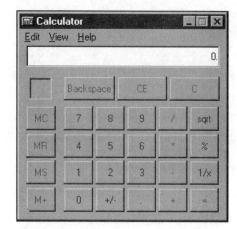

Figure 38. *The Calculator*

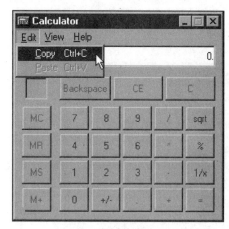

Figure 39. *Copying a result.*

Figure 40. *The Phone Dialer.*

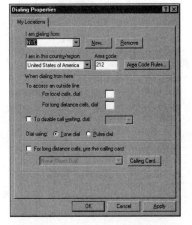

Figure 41. *Check the dialing properties.*

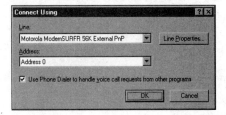

Figure 42. *The Connect Using dialog box.*

Setting Up the Phone Dialer

You can use the Phone Dialer accessory to have your modem dial phone numbers. Before you dial, though, you should check and modify the phone settings to make sure Phone Dialer knows your area code, country code, and how to access an outside line.

1. Open the Phone Dialer accessory. The Phone Dialer window opens. **(Figure 40)**

2. From the Tools menu, select Dialing Properties.

3. Make any necessary changes on the Dialing Properties dialog box. **(Figure 41)**

4. Click OK.

✔ Tips

■ You must have a modem installed in order to use Phone Dialer.

■ To modify modem settings from within Phone Dialer, choose Connect Using from the Tools menu and then click Line Properties. **(Figure 42)**

Dialing a Number with Phone Dialer

1. Open the Phone Dialer accessory.

2. In the Number to dial field, enter the phone number, including the area code. **(Figure 43)** You can either type the numbers on your keyboard or click the numbers in the Phone Dialer window.

3. Click Dial. If the number you've entered is not one of your speed call numbers, enter a name for the call tracking log and click OK. **(Figure 44)**

4. When the Call Status dialog box appears, pick up the handset on your telephone and click Talk. **(Figure 45)**

5. If no one answers, if the line is busy, or when you are ready to end your call, click Hang Up.

✔ Tips

■ You can copy a telephone number from another application and paste it into the Number to dial field.

■ You don't need to enter the area code if it is the same as that at your current location.

Figure 43. *Enter a number to dial.*

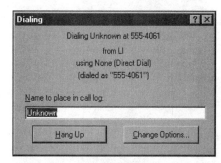

Figure 44. *Type in a name for the phone log.*

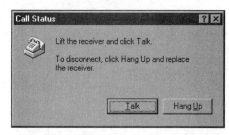

Figure 45. *Pick up the telephone handset and click the Talk button*

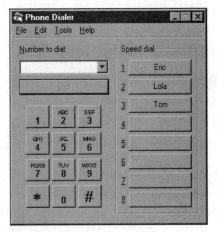

Figure 46. *Click an empty speed dial button.*

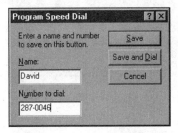

Figure 47. *Enter info for the button.*

Defining the Speed Dial Buttons

You can store the phone numbers you dial most often in the eight speed dial buttons. **(Figure 46)** Then with a single mouse click, you can have Phone Dialer instantly dial the number associated with that button.

1. Click an empty speed dial button. The Program Speed Dial dialog box appears. **(Figure 47)**
2. In the Name field, type the name of the person or company.
3. In the Number to dial field, type the phone number, including area code.
4. Click Save.

✔ Tip

■ To dial someone on your speed dial list, just click the appropriate button.

Defining the Speed Dial Buttons

Playing Audio CDs in your CD Player

If your machine has a CD-ROM drive, a sound card, and speakers, or at least headphones, you may be able to play music CDs with the Windows CD Player.

1. Put the music CD in the CD-ROM drive.

2. Start the CD Player accessory. It's on the Entertainment submenu of the Accessories menu. **(Figure 48)**

3. Press the Play button to start the music. **(Figure 48)**

4. Press the other buttons on the CD Player window the same way you'd press the buttons on a real CD player.

✔ Tips

■ If you try this procedure and you do not hear music, you may need to use a cable to connect the audio output from the CD-ROM player with the audio input of the sound card.

■ With the Edit Play List command on the Disc menu, you can enter the name of the CD and the track titles. **(Figure 49)**

Play button

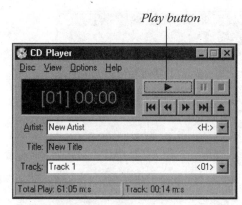

Figure 48. *The CD Player*

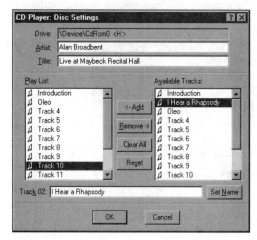

Figure 49. *You can enter your own track lists.*

Disks, Folders, and Files

In this Chapter...

You will learn about the three entities within your system in which information is stored: disks, folders, and files.

You will learn to open disks and folders to view their contents, and work with the folders, subfolders, and files that you find inside.

Understanding how to copy and move folders and files will let you make backup copies of your work and move programs and documents from one disk to another or from one computer to another. Learning to delete folders and files will let you clear out old junk and recover clogged space. And creating new folders gives you the chance to organize your work in ways that will keep it easy to find.

You'll also learn two very handy techniques that will make it easy for you to come back to documents with which you worked with recently or reopen a resource to which you'd like ready access.

In this Chapter

Opening a Disk to View its Folders and Files

The files in your system are organized into folders on your disks. To get to a folder or file to copy, move, delete, or rename it, you must open a disk.

1. On the Windows desktop, double-click the My Computer icon.
   (Figure 1)

2. In the My Computer window, double-click the icon of the disk that you want to open. **(Figures 2–3)**

3. If you want to open a second window so you can drag files back and forth, repeat steps 1 and 2.

✔ Tips

■ If a disk or folder icon is underlined, or if it becomes underlined when you move the mouse pointer onto it, you can single-click the icon rather than double-click it. **(Figure 4)**

■ To set Windows so that you can single-click disks, folders, and files, choose Folder Options from the View menu of the My Computer window, and choose Web Style.

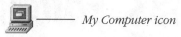

My Computer icon

Figure 1. *Double-click My Computer.*

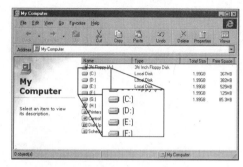

Figure 2. *Double-click a disk icon.*

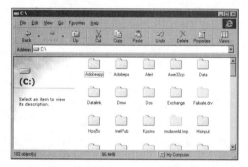

Figure 3. *The folders on the disk appear.*

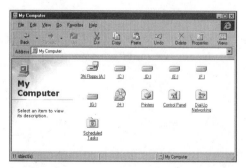

Figure 4. *You can single-click icons that are underlined.*

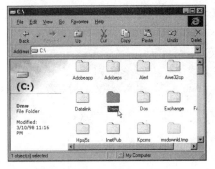

Figure 5. *Double-click a folder icon.*

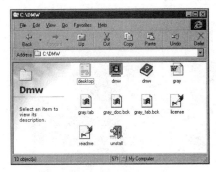

Figure 6. *The folder's files appear.*

Figure 7. *Choose Auto Arrange.*

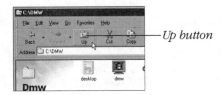

— *Up button*

Figure 8. *Click the Up button.*

Opening a Folder

After you open a disk, you can open the folders on the disk.

> Double-click a folder icon to open the folder. **(Figure 5–6)**
>
> *or*
>
> Click the folder icon if it is underlined.

✔ Tips

■ You can choose whether the folder you open will display in the current window or whether each folder you open will display in its own window.

■ To have the folder and file icons within windows line up neatly, choose Arrange Icons from the View menu, and then choose Auto Arrange from the submenu. **(Figure 7)**

Exiting From a Folder

> Click the Up button on the toolbar. **(Figure 8)**
>
> *or*
>
> If a new window has opened to display the folder, close the new window.
> **(Figure 9)**

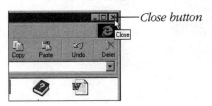

— *Close button*

Figure 9. *Click the close button.*

Opening a Folder

Navigating Backward and Forward

Windows 98 lets you use the same techniques to navigate your system's disks, folders, and files that you use to navigate Web sites on the Internet.

To use these techniques, you must have Windows set to open successive folders in the same window rather than in separate windows.

Click the Back button to backtrack to the previous folder. **(Figure 10)**

✔ Tips

■ After you click the Back button and move backward to the previous folder, the Forward button becomes available so you can move forward again to the next folder. **(Figure 11)**

■ To return to a specific previous folder, click the down arrow button next to the Back button. **(Figure 12)**

■ You can also pull down the Address list on the Address toolbar and click any disk or folder on the list. **(Figure 13)**

Back button

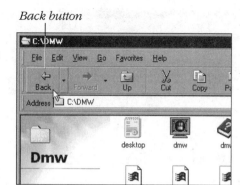

Figure 10. *Click the Back button*

Forward button

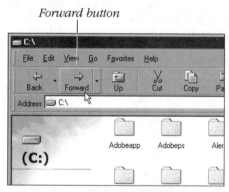

Figure 11. *Click the Forward button.*

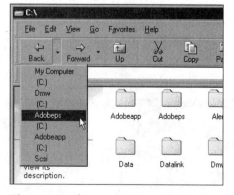

Figure 12. *Choose a previous destination.*

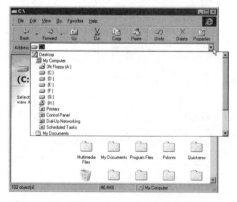

Figure 13. *Choose from the Address list.*

Views button

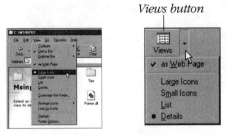

Figure 14. *View menu.*   **Figure 15**. *Views button.*

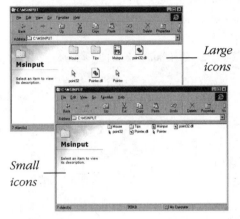

Large icons

Small icons

Figure 16. *Large Icons view and Small Icons siew.*

List

Details

Figure 17. *List view and Details view.*

Changing Views

Windows gives you a choice of four different views that a window can use to display the contents of a disk or folder.

Choose a view from the View menu.
(Figure 14)

or

Click the Views button on the toolbar to switch to the next view.
(Figure 15)

✔ Tips

■ You can also click the down-arrow button next to the Views button on the toolbar to pull down a menu of views.
(Figure 15)

View	Description
Large Icons	The folders and files in a folder are displayed as large icons. **(Figure 16)**
Small Icons	The folders and files are displayed as small icons in rows. **(Figure 16)**
List	The folders and files are displayed as small icons in columns. **(Figure 17)**
Details	The folders and files are displayed in a column. Additional columns list the size, type, and date and time last modified. Click a column heading button to sort the entries according to the column. Click the Date button to sort by date, for example. Click the same button again to reverse the sort order. **(Figure 17)**

Changing Views

Checking the Properties of a Folder or File

1. Click the folder or file with the right mouse button. **(Figure 18)**

2. From the shortcut menu, choose Properties. **(Figure 19)**

3. Click Cancel or OK after you finish viewing the properties sheet. **(Figure 20)**

✔ Tips

■ The properties sheet of a folder shows the total number and the cumulative size of all the files in the folder.

■ On the properties sheet of a file, you can change the file's attributes. Read-only prevents the file from being modified. Hidden removes the file from the display of files unless you specifically choose to see hidden files.

■ Certain file types have additional tabs in the Properties window. Click these tabs to see the additional properties.

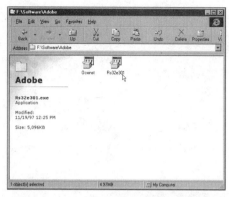

Figure 18. *Right-click the folder or file.*

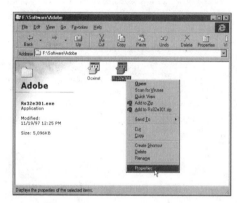

Figure 19. *Choose Properties from the shortcut menu.*

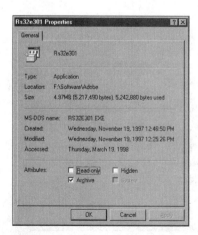

Figure 20. *The Properties sheet.*

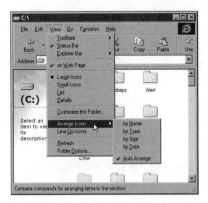

Figure 21. *Choose Arrange Icons from the View menu.*

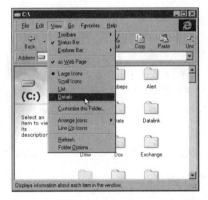

Figure 22. *Choose Details from the View menu.*

Sorting Folders and Files

1. From the View menu, choose Arrange Icons. **(Figure 21)**

or

Right-click anywhere within the folder window and choose Arrange Icons from the shortcut menu.

2. On the Arrange Icons submenu, choose By Name, By Type, By Size, or By Date.

or

1. From the View menu, choose Details. **(Figure 22)**

2. Click the button at the top of a column to sort the entries according to that column. **(Figure 23)**

✔ Tip

■ You can click the button at the top of a column again to switch between an ascending and descending sort order.

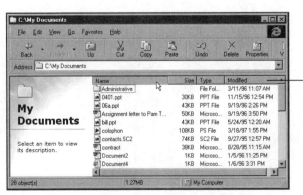

—*Click a column-top button.*

Figure 23. *Click a column heading to sort the entries according to that column.*

Opening a Second Disk or Folder

To perform some of the procedures on the next few pages, you'll need to drag files from one window to another. Here's a quick and easy way to arrange windows on the screen.

1. Open a disk or folder from the My Computer window. **(Figure 24)**

2. Return to My Computer and open a second disk or folder. **(Figure 25)**

3. Right-click an empty part of the taskbar (don't click on a button or icon on the taskbar) and choose Tile Windows Vertically from the shortcut menu. Windows will display the open windows side by side. **(Figures 26–27)**

✔ Tips

■ Choose Tile Windows Horizontally to have the windows arrange one above the other.

■ All open windows will be tiled. If an extra window becomes tiled, too (if a third windows was open on the desktop), minimize that window and then choose Tile Windows Horizontally again.

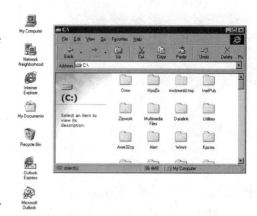

Figure 24. *Open a disk or folder.*

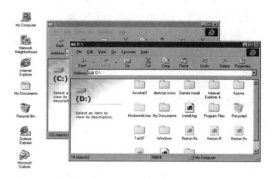

Figure 25. *Open a second disk or folder from My Computer.*

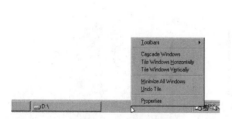

Figure 26. *Right-click the Taskbar.*

Figure 27. *Windows tiled vertically.*

Click the first file and press Shift.

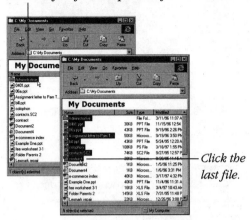

Figure 28. *Click the first file, hold down the Shift key, and click the last file.*

— *Click the last file.*

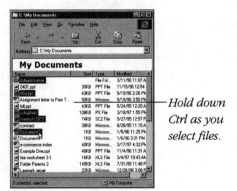

Figure 29. *Hold down Ctrl while you click files.*

— *Hold down Ctrl as you select files.*

Figure 30. *Draw a selection box around icons.*

Selecting Multiple Folders and Files

Copying or moving files one by one is tedious, so Windows lets you select multiple files and handle them all at once.

1. Click the first folder or file to select.

2. Press and hold down the Shift key.

3. Click the last folder or file to select. The files in between are selected also. **(Figure 28)**

or

1. Click the first folder or file to select.

2. Press and hold down the Ctrl key.

3. Click each additional folder or file that you want to add to the selection group. **(Figure 29)**

If the Windows desktop style is "Web Style," follow this procedure instead:

1. Place the mouse pointer on the first folder or file without clicking and wait until it is highlighted.

2. Press and hold down the Shift key.

3. Place the mouse pointer on the last folder or file without clicking and wait until it is highlighted.

or

1. Place the mouse pointer on the first folder or file without clicking and wait until it is highlighted.

2. Press and hold down the Ctrl key.

3. Place the mouse pointer on each additional file to select and wait until it is highlighted.

✔ Tip

■ You can also use the mouse pointer to draw a selection box around the folders or files you want. **(Figure 30)**

Copying or Moving Folders or Files

1. Select the folders or files to move. **(Figure 31)**

2. To copy the folders or files, drag them to another window. **(Figure 32)**

or

To move the folders or files, press and hold down the Shift key as you drag them.

✔ Tips

■ When you are copying rather than moving folders or files, a plus sign appears next to the icons. **(Figure 33)**

■ You can also press the right mouse button as you drag the icons to a different window. After the drag is completed, Windows will ask whether you want to move or copy the folders or files. **(Figure 34)**

Figure 31. *Select folders or files.*

Figure 32. *Drag them to another window.*

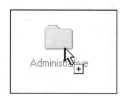

Figure 33. *The copying icon.*

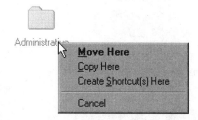

Figure 34. *Choose Move Here or Copy Here from the shortcut menu.*

Copying or Moving Folders and Files

Figure 35. *The Find submenu.*

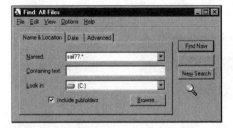

Figure 36. *Enter part of a file name.*

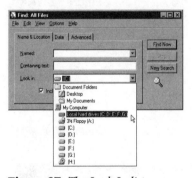

Figure 37. *The Look In list.*

Figure 38. *The "found" folders or files.*

Finding a Folder or File

1. Click the Start button.

2. On the Start menu, choose Find.

3. On the Find submenu, choose Files or Folders. **(Figure 35)**

4. On the Find dialog box, enter the file or folder name or part of the name. You can use question marks and asterisks to mean any letter or group of letters when specifying a file or folder name. **(Figure 36)**

5. From the Look In list, select the hard drive you want to search or, if you have multiple hard drives, select "Local hard drives" to search them all. **(Figure 37)**

6. Click Find Now.

7. On the list of "found" files that appears within the dialog box, double-click any file to open it in the application in which it was created. **(Figure 38)**

✔ Tips

■ You can drag items from the "found" list to move or copy them.

■ To look in a particular drive or folder, click the Browse button, click the drive or folder on the "Browse for Folder" list, and click OK.

■ Make sure the Include Subfolders check box is checked so Find will search the folders within the selected drive or folder.

■ If a search comes up empty, you can click the New Search button and then enter different search criteria.

Finding a Folder or File

Deleting Folders or Files

Select the folders or files to delete and press the Delete key on the keyboard.

or

Drag the folder or file icons to the Recycle Bin. **(Figure 39)**

or

Select the folders or files and choose Delete from the File menu. **(Figure 40)**

or

Click a folder or file with the right mouse button and choose Delete from the shortcut menu.

✔ Tips

■ To permanently remove files you have deleted, click the Recycle Bin icon with the right mouse button and choose Empty Recycle Bin from the shortcut menu. **(Figure 41)**

■ When you delete a folder, you also delete all the files in the folder.

Retrieving Deleted Folders or Files

The folders and files you delete are sent to the Recycle Bin.

1. Double-click the Recycle Bin.

2. Select the folders or files to retrieve.

3. Click the Restore link.

or

From the File menu, choose Restore. **(Figure 42)**

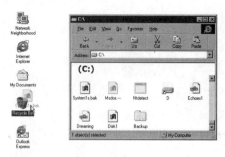

Figure 39. *Drag the icon to the Recycle Bin.*

Figure 40. *The File menu.*

Figure 41. *The shortcut menu.*

The Restore link.

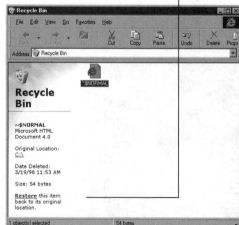

Figure 42. *The Recycle Bin.*

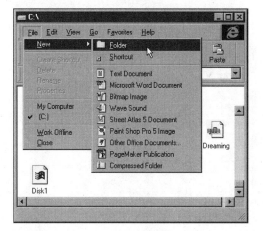

Figure 43. *Choose Folder from the New submenu.*

Enter a new folder name.

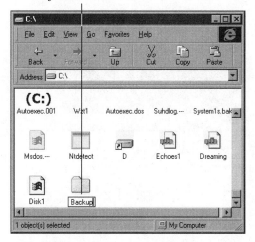

Figure 44. *Enter a new folder name.*

Creating a New Folder

1. Open the disk or folder in which you want to create a new folder.

2. From the File menu, choose New.

3. On the New submenu, choose Folder. **(Figure 43)**

4. When the new folder appears, type over the currently highlighted text "Folder Name" to replace it with the name you want. Remember, you can use a long file name that can include spaces. **(Figure 44)**

✔ **Tip**

■ You can also right-click the background of a folder or file window and then choose New from the shortcut menu.

Renaming a Folder or File

1. Click a folder name or file name.
(Figure 45)

2. Wait a second or two.

3. Click the folder name or file name
again. This places the name in a text
box highlighted and ready for editing.
(Figure 46)

4. Type over the currently highlighted
name, or edit the name, and then press
Enter. **(Figure 47)**

✔ Tip

■ You can also select a folder or file and
then press F2 to begin renaming it.

Figure 45. *Click a folder or file name and
pause.*

Figure 46. *Click again so you can edit the
name.*

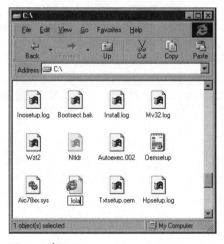

Figure 47. *Enter a new name.*

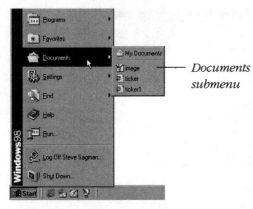

Documents submenu

Figure 48. *The Documents submenu.*

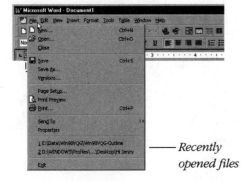

Recently opened files

Figure 49. *The recently opened file list on the Microsoft Word File menu.*

Opening a Recently Opened Document

1. Click the Start button.

2. From the Start menu, choose Documents. **(Figure 48)**

3. On the Documents submenu, which lists the files you've recently used, choose a file.

✔ Tips

■ Many applications have a list of recently opened files on the File menu. **(Figure 49)**

■ You can also click "My Documents" on the Documents submenu to open the My Documents folder on your system.

Creating a Desktop Shortcut to a Folder or File

A shortcut is a copy of an icon that you've placed on the Windows desktop or in another folder. Double-clicking the shortcut performs the same function as double-clicking the original icon. You can place shortcuts to various files in a single folder to organize your work by project, date, or some other way.

1. Select a disk, folder or file. **(Figure 50)**

2. Press and hold the right mouse button as you drag the folder or file icon to the desktop.

3. On the shortcut menu that appears, choose Create Shortcut(s) Here. **(Figure 51)** Now, if you want, you can move the shortcut to a folder.

✔ Tips

■ A shortcut icon looks like the original icon except that it has a shortcut arrow at the lower-left corner. **(Figure 52)**

■ To conserve screen space, you can delete the words "Shortcut to" in the shortcut icon's title. The shortcut arrow at the lower-left corner identifies the icon as a shortcut.

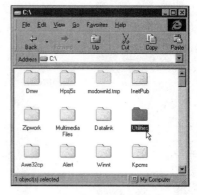

Figure 50. *Select an icon.*

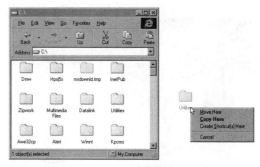

Figure 51. *Drag the icon with the right mouse button pressed.*

Figure 52. *The shortcut.*

Exploring Your Computer

In this Chapter...

You will learn about a special tool that you can use in Windows to accomplish all the same tasks that you learned in the previous chapter. This tool, the Windows Explorer, offers a unique way to view the resources on your computer and handle basic system management tasks, such as moving files among disks, renaming folders, and choosing printers.

You can probably get by without ever learning about the Windows Explorer because you can use other features of Windows to do what the Explorer can do. But the Windows Explorer makes many tasks a little easier because of the way it presents and organizes information in a single window.

The "Explorer-style" view of information is also used by a number of Windows programs, so it's a good feature to become familiar with. Knowing about the Explorer can help your work both now and down the road.

In this Chapter

What Is the Explorer?

The Windows Explorer is a special tool that gives you a double-barreled view of the resources of your computer, such as its disks, folders, and printers. **(Figure 1)**

Unlike a standard window, the Explorer is split into two side-by-side panes. The left pane shows an outline-style list of all the resources available to you. If you select a resource, the right pane shows you its contents. For example, if you select a disk icon in the left pane by clicking it, you see the folders on the disks in the right pane. If you click the Printers folder on the left, you will see the printer icons on the right. You can also click a folder in the left pane and see the folder's files in the right pane.

The right pane is just like the window that opens when you click My Computer or Network Neighborhood. It has all the same attributes and capabilities. You can drag folders and files from it to another window, for example, and you can choose among the four views by clicking the Views button. You can apply all the knowledge you gained from the previous chapter to using the right pane of the Explorer.

If you are connected to a network, the Explorer also lets you view and work with the resources out on the network.

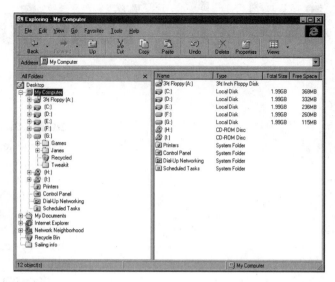

Figure 1. *The Windows Explorer window.*

What Is the Explorer?

Figure 2. *Right-click the My Computer icon.*

Figure 3. *Choose Explore from the shortcut menu.*

Starting the Explorer

1. On the Windows desktop, click the My Computer icon with the right mouse button. **(Figure 2)**

2. From the shortcut menu, choose Explore. **(Figures 3–4)**

✔ Tips

■ Even though some of the objects in the left pane are clearly computers, disks, and printers, the Explorer labels the left pane "All Folders." Everything in the right pane is the contents of a folder. **Figure 5**, on the next page, shows the Explorer window in full detail.

■ Click any object in the left pane to view its contents in the right pane.

■ You can open multiple copies of the Explorer in separate windows by repeating the steps above.

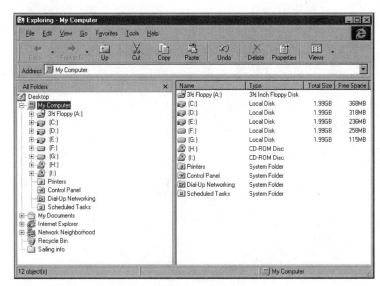

Figure 4. *The Windows Explorer opens.*

The Explorer Window

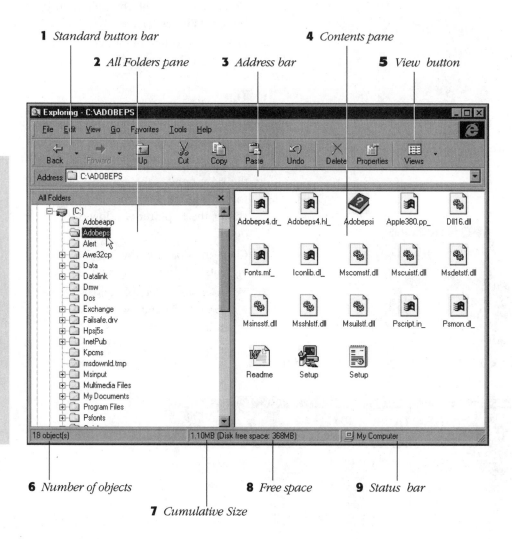

1 *Standard button bar*

2 *All Folders pane*

3 *Address bar*

4 *Contents pane*

5 *View button*

6 *Number of objects*

7 *Cumulative Size*

8 *Free space*

9 *Status bar*

Figure 5. *The Windows Explorer.*

1 Standard button bar

Click the buttons on the Standard button bar to navigate through the system, work with files, or change the view.

2 All Folders pane

Displays the resources of your system and your network as an outline-stuctured list. Click any folder in this pane to display its contents in the right pane.

3 Address bar

Shows the name of the resource that is selected in the All Folders pane. Enter a path name or a resource name to jump quickly to that disk, folder, or resource.

4 Contents pane

Shows the contents of the selected folder in the All Folders pane. The Contents pane displays folders and files in one of four views: Large Icons, Small Icons, List, and Details. You can change among views by clicking the View button.

5 View button

Click this button to cycle to the next view or click the down arrow next to this button to open a menu of views.

6 Number of objects

Displays the number of objects in the currently selected folder in the All Folders pane. If you select one or more objects in the Contents pane, you see the number of objects that you've selected.

7 Cumulative Size

Reports the size of the files in the current folder. If the folder has subfolders, this number shows the cumulative size of all the files in all the subfolders. If you select folders and files in the Contents pane, this figure reports the cumulative size of the selected files.

8 Free space

Reports the free space that is available on the selected the disk.

9 Status bar

Provides information about the selected or open objects in the Folders and Contents panes. Also displays the Internet Zone.

Revealing the Folders in an Object

When a folder in the left pane is preceded by a plus sign, it contains subfolders that you can reveal. The subfolders are already visible when a folder is preceded by a minus sign. A folder without a plus or a minus in front of it has no folders inside. Remember, a folder can be a disk, or a resource on the network, such as a network printer.

1. In the left pane, click the plus sign in front of a folder to reveal its subfolders. **(Figures 6–7)**

or

Double-click a folder that is preceded by plus sign.

2. Click a folder icon to display its contents in the right pane. **(Figure 8)**

✔ Tips

■ You can also move the highlight to a folder with the arrow keys and press the Plus key on the numeric keypad to reveal the subfolders in a folder.

■ To open a folder in its own window, click the folder with the right mouse button and then choose Open from the shortcut menu. Then you can easily drag icons from the Explorer to the other window and vice versa.

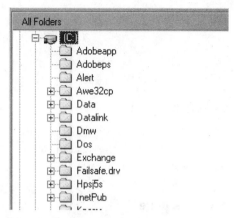

Figure 6. *The outline-style list of folders.*

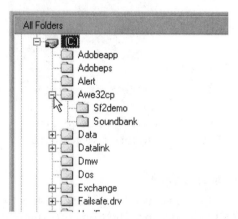

Figure 7. *Clicking a plus sign reveals subfolders.*

Figure 8. *Click a folder to see its contents in the right pane.*

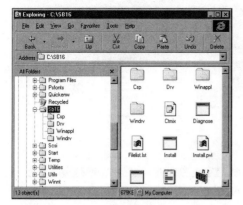

Figure 9. *Click the minus sign in front of a folder to hide subfolders.*

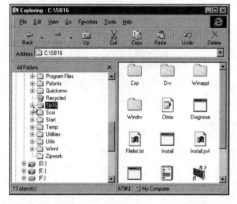

Figure 10. *The subfolders are no longer visible.*

Hiding the Folders in an Object

Click the minus sign in front of a folder to hide its subfolders.
(Figures 9–10)

or

Double-click an object whose subfolders are visible.

✔ Tip

■ You can also move the highlight to a folder with the arrow keys and press the Minus key on the numeric keypad to hide the subfolders in a folder.

Switching to the Explorer

You don't have to use the Explorer when you first open a disk or folder. After you use My Computer to open a disk or folder, you can view the contents of a particular folder or subfolder in the Explorer.

1. On the Windows desktop, double-click the My Computer icon. The My Computer window opens. **(Figure 11)**

2. In the My Computer window, click the the icon of a disk or a folder on a disk with the right mouse button and choose Explore from the shortcut menu. **(Figures 12–13)**

✔ **Tip**

■ You can always use the Explorer to investigate any folder on your system by right-clicking the folder and choosing Explore from the shortcut menu.

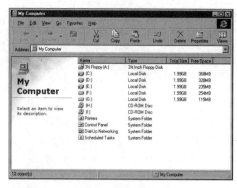

Figure 11. *The My Computer window.*

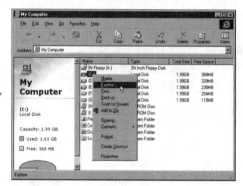

Figure 12. *Right-click an icon and choose Explore from the shortcut menu.*

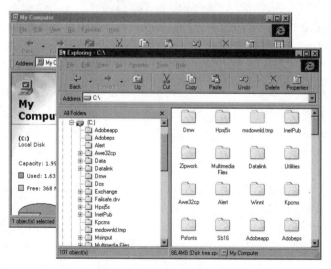

Figure 13. *The Explorer opens in a window.*

Printing Files

In this Chapter...

You will learn to handle that cantankerous contraption called a printer. While everything else in your computer happens quietly, quickly, and electronically, a printer squawks, squeaks, jams, and beeps. Even laser printers, from which pages emerge relatively quietly, have their disagreeable moments.

To produce paper copies of the pages you see on the screen, you'll need to choose a printer in Windows and learn to manage the print queue, which holds print jobs and delivers them one by one to your printer.

You'll learn to view the queue, pause the queue, cancel specific documents, and change the order of the jobs that are waiting to be printed. You'll also learn to check the wait at all the printers on your network so you can find a printer that is just waiting for some files from you.

Selecting a Default Printer

If you have more than one printer
connected to your computer (a black and
white laser printer and a color inkjet
printer, for example), you can set one of
the printers as the default printer so you
won't have to choose a printer each time
you print.

1. From the Start menu, choose Settings.

2. On the Settings submenu, choose
Printers. **(Figure 1)**

3. In the Printers window, click a printer
icon with the right mouse button.
(Figure 2)

4. From the shortcut menu, choose Set as
Default. A check mark appears next to
the default printer. **(Figures 3–4)**

✔ Tips

■ If you have only one printer, it is set as
the default printer automatically.

■ Even though you've chosen a
particular default printer, you can still
choose another printer at the time you
print a particular file.

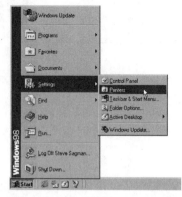

Figure 1. *Choose Printers from
the Settings submenu.*

Figure 2. *Click a printer icon with the
right mouse button.*

Figure 3. *Choose Set as Default.*

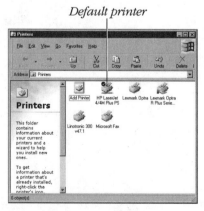

Figure 4. *A check mark appears next to the
default printer.*

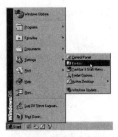

Figure 5. *Choose Printers from the Settings submenu.*

Figure 6. *Choose Properties from the shortcut menu.*

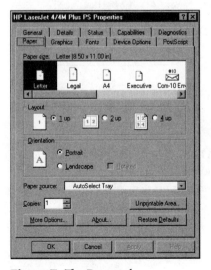

Figure 7. *The Paper tab.*

Changing the Printer's Properties

Each printer has a set of properties that determine how it will print your work. Changing the properties lets you choose a different paper source (manual feed rather than paper tray, for example), or an alternate print resolution.

1. From the Start menu, choose Settings.

2. On the Settings submenu, choose Printers. **(Figure 5)**

3. In the Printers window, click a printer icon with the right mouse button.

4. From the shortcut menu, choose Properties. **(Figure 6)**

5. In the Properties dialog box, change settings on the various tabs and then click OK. **(Figure 7)**

✔ Tip

■ The capabilities of the printer determine the properties you see on the Properties dialog box. A printer with two paper trays for different types of paper will have a setting that allows you to change trays, for example.

About the Print Queue

When you send a document to a printer, the print queue for the printer intercepts and holds the document, and then feeds it to the printer as the printer is ready for it. Each printer has its own print queue. Because the queue takes care of the printing, it leaves your programs free to do other work.

When you are connected to a network, the print queue for a printer absorbs print jobs from everyone who shares the printer. It then feeds the documents in order to the shared printer.

Viewing a Print Queue

After you send one or more documents to a printer, you can check the printer's queue to learn about the status of your print job.

Double-click the printer icon that appears at the right end of the Taskbar when documents are printing. **(Figure 8)**

or

1. Double-click the My Computer icon and then double-click the Printers icon in the My Computer window. **(Figure 9)**

2. Double-click a printer icon in the Printers window to open its print queue. **(Figure 10)**

✔ Tip

■ To check the number of documents in the print queue without opening the queue, place the mouse pointer on the printer icon in the taskbar *but do not click.* **(Figure 11)**

The printer icon.

Figure 8. *Double-click the printer icon on the Taskbar.*

Figure 9. *Double-click the Printers icon.*

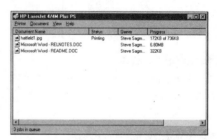

Figure 10. *The print queue for a printer*

Figure 11. *Put the pointer on the printer icon* but do not click *to check the pending documents at a printer.*

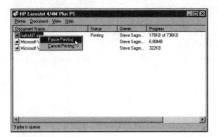

Figure 12. *Click a document name with the right mouse button.*

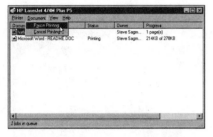

Figure 13. *From the Document menu, choose Pause Printing.*

Figure 14. *Choose Pause Printing from the Printer menu.*

Pausing a Document

When you pause a document in the print queue, the documents that follow on the list will begin printing.

1. While viewing the print queue for a printer, click a document name with the right mouse button. **(Figure 12)** *See Viewing a Print Queue on the opposite page.*

2. From the shortcut menu, choose Pause Printing.

   or

1. While viewing the print queue for a printer, click a document name.

2. From the Document menu, choose Pause Printing. **(Figure 13)**

✔ Tips

■ To resume printing of a document, follow the same steps. This time, though, clear the check mark next to Pause Printing.

■ To pause the printing of all documents, choose Pause Printing from the Printer menu in the queue window, instead. **(Figure 14)**

Canceling a Document

1. While viewing the print queue for a printer, click a document name with the right mouse button.

2. From the shortcut menu, choose Cancel Printing. **(Figure 15)**

or

1. While viewing the print queue for a printer, click a document name.

2. From the Document menu, choose Cancel Printing. **(Figure 16)**

✔ **Tips**

■ To remove all documents from the print queue, choose Purge Print Documents from the Printer menu. **(Figure 17)**

■ You can only cancel documents that you have the right to cancel, such as documents you've sent. Sorry, you cannot cancel documents printed by others on the network to push your jobs ahead.

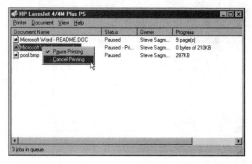

Figure 15. *Choose Cancel Printing from the shortcut menu.*

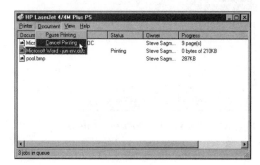

Figure 16. *Choose Cancel Printing from the Document menu.*

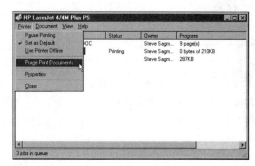

Figure 17. *Choose Purge Print Documents from the Printer menu.*

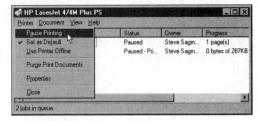

Figure 18. *Choose Pause Printer from the Printer menu.*

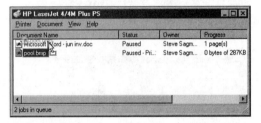

Figure 19. *Drag documents up or down on the list.*

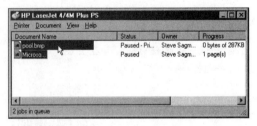

Figure 20. *Choose Pause Printing a second time to resume printing.*

Changing the Order of Print Jobs

1. While viewing the print queue for a printer, choose Pause Printing from the Printer menu. **(Figure 18)**

2. Drag and drop documents up or down on the list of queued documents to change the order of waiting documents. **(Figure 19)**

3. Resume printing by choosing Pause Printing again from the Printer menu. **(Figure 20)**

Changing the Order of Print Jobs

Checking the Wait at All Printers

If you have more than one printer attached to your computer, or if you are on a network that has several printers available, you can check the number of documents in the various printer queues.

1. Double-click the My Computer icon.

2. In the My Computer window, double-click the Printers icon. **(Figure 21)**

3. In the Printers window, switch to Details view by clicking the Views button.

or

From the View menu, choose Details. **(Figure 22)**

✔ **Tip**

■ The Status column in Details view tells you which printers are paused, offline, or in need of user intervention (time to add paper or fix a jam). **(Figure 23)**

Figure 21. *Double-click the Printers icon.*

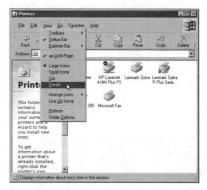

Figure 22. *Switch to Details view.*

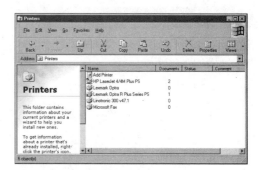

Figure 23. *The Status column can tell you if a printer needs your assistance.*

Part 2
Managing
Your Computer

Part 2
Managing
Your Computer

Changing Windows Settings

In this Chapter...

You will learn to change the look of the Windows desktop and many of the items that appear on it, such as the icons and the text captions.

You also will learn to restructure the Start menu so you can get to the programs you need quickly and easily. You can add new programs, delete others, and reorganize program icons into folders that have a structure that makes sense to you.

Finally, you'll learn to view, add, and remove fonts that will work in all your programs, and to customize the way the mouse and sound system works.

Changing the Background of the Desktop

1. Click the desktop with the right mouse button and choose Properties from the shortcut menu. **(Figure 1)**

2. On the Background tab of the Properties dialog box, choose a Wallpaper from the Wallpaper list. You can also click the Patterns button to choose a pattern for the desktop background. **(Figures 2)**

3. Choose Apply to see your choice appear on the desktop immediately.

✔ Tips

■ When you choose a wallpaper, you can also choose an option on the Display drop-down list. "Tile" fills the desktop by repeating the wallpaper. "Stretch" fills the desktop by stretching the wallpaper. **(Figure 3)**

■ To remove the wallpaper, choose None at the top of the Wallpaper list.

Figure 1. *Right-click the desktop.*

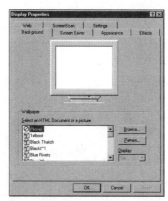

Figure 2. *The Display Properties dialog box.*

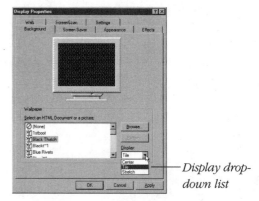

—Display drop-down list

Figure 3. *The Display drop-down list.*

Changing the Background of the Desktop

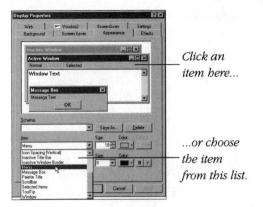

Click an item here...

...or choose the item from this list.

Figure 4. *Click an element to select it for editing.*

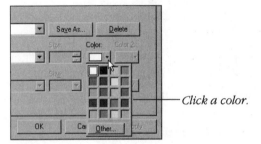

Click a color.

Figure 5. *Choose a color from the color drop-down palette.*

Figure 6. *Save your new color scheme by giving it a name.*

Changing the Screen Colors

1. Click the desktop with the right mouse button and choose Properties from the shortcut menu.

2. On the Appearance tab of the Display Properties dialog box, click an on-screen element on the sample shown in the top half of the dialog box or select an element from the Item drop-down list. **(Figure 4)**

3. On the Appearance tab, click the button that shows the current color to pull down a palette of colors. **(Figure 5)**

4. Click one of the colors on the palette and then click Apply to see the change immediately.

5. Repeat steps 2–4 until you have made all the color changes you want.

6. Save the new color scheme by clicking Save As and then entering a name for the color scheme in the Save Scheme dialog box. **(Figure 6)**

7. Click OK to accept the current color scheme.

✔ Tips

- If you've chosen a wallpaper for the desktop, you will see the background color only around the titles of the icons on the desktop.

- Make sure you choose a color for the background that contrasts with the color of text under the icons, or change the color of the icon text.

Changing the Size of On-Screen Items

Many on-screen items, such as title bars and scroll bars, can be resized to your liking. You can enlarge the caption buttons for example (the Minimize, Maximize, and Close buttons at the upper-right corner of each window) to make them easier to click.

1. Click the desktop with the right mouse button and choose Properties from the shortcut menu.

2. On the Appearance tab of the Display Properties dialog box, click an on-screen element on the sample or choose an item from the Item list. If the item can be resized, you'll see the current size in the Size textbox next to the item name. Otherwise, the Size box will be blank. **(Figure 7)**

3. Click the up or down arrows next to the Size box to increase or decrease the size of the item. **(Figure 8)**

4. Click Apply to see the change immediately or click OK to accept the change and close the Display Properties dialog box.

✔ Tips

■ Before you start changing the size of on-screen elements, you may want to take a look at some of the preset color schemes. Some are labeled large and extra large for high resolution displays. **(Figure 9)**

■ If you find a preset color scheme that provides font choices you like, you can then alter particular colors to your satisfaction.

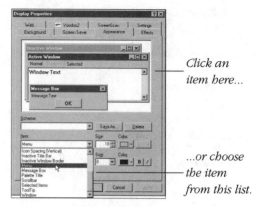

Click an item here...

...or choose the item from this list.

Figure 7. *Choose an item to edit.*

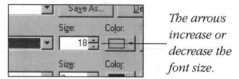

The arrows increase or decrease the font size.

Figure 8. *The font size control.*

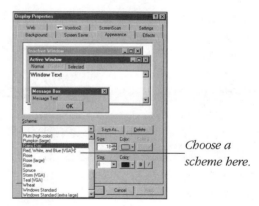

Choose a scheme here.

Figure 9. *Choose an existing display scheme.*

Figure 10. *Select a font from the font drop-down list.*

Figure 11. *Double-click the Display icon.*

Changing the On-Screen Fonts

You can change the style, size, and color of the text used in windows, menus, message boxes, and even on the desktop itself.

1. Click the desktop with the right mouse button and choose Properties from the shortcut menu.

2. On the Appearance tab of the Display Properties dialog box, click an on-screen element on the sample or choose an item from the Item list. If the text associated with the item can be modified, you'll see entries in the Font, Size and Color controls (the bottom row of controls on the Appearance tab). **(Figure 10)**

3. Make selections on the Font and Size pull-down lists, and then click the color button if you want to choose a different color.

4. Click the **B** and *I* buttons if you want to boldface or italicize the text.

5. Click Apply to see the change immediately or click OK to accept the change and close the Display Properties dialog box.

✔ Tip

■ You can also get to the Display Properties dialog box by opening the Control Panel from the Start menu and then double-clicking the Display icon in the Control Panel window. **(Figure 11)**

Changing the Screen Resolution

Resolution is the number of dots, or pixels, displayed on your screen. The lowest common resolution is 640 across by 480 down, but some systems are capable of 800 x 600, 1024 x 768, or even 1280 x 1024. The higher the resolution, the sharper everything looks.

1. Click the desktop with the right mouse button and choose Properties from the shortcut menu.

2. On the Settings tab of the Properties dialog box, drag the Screen area slider left or right to change the resolution. **(Figure 12)**

3. Choose one of the selections on the Colors drop-down list. **(Figure 13)**

4. Click OK to see the change immediately.

✔ Tips

■ Click Advanced to see settings that pertain to your particular video card and monitor. **(Figure 14)**

■ The Settings tab will only display the choices that your video system can provide.

■ When you choose the *Show settings icon on task bar* option, a display settings icon appears on the Taskbar. Click this icon to get a pop-up menu of your system's display settings options. **(Figure 15)**

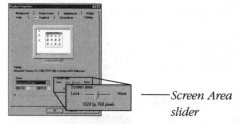

———*Screen Area slider*

Figure 12. *Drag the Screen Area slider to change the resolution.*

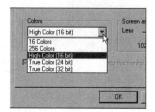

Figure 13. *Select the number of colors from the Colors drop-down list.*

Figure 14. *Advanced properties.*

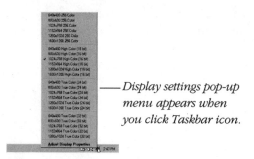

———*Display settings pop-up menu appears when you click Taskbar icon.*

Figure 15. *Taskbar display settings icon and pop-up menu.*

Changing the Screen Resolution

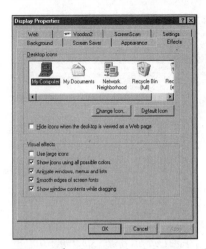

Figure 16. *Click the check boxes on the Effects tab to enable or disable special visual effects on the Windows desktop.*

Changing Visual Effects

Special visual effects settings are available on the Effects tab of the Display Properties dialog box.

1. Click the desktop with the right mouse button and choose Properties from the shortcut menu.

2. On the Effects tab, click the Visual Effects check boxes to turn the effects on or off. **(Figure 16)**

✔ Tips

■ Some effects are available only when your display is set to High Color on the Settings tab of the Display Properties dialog box.

Uses a larger set of icons to display programs, folders, and files on the desktop.

Windows, menus, and lists slide into view.

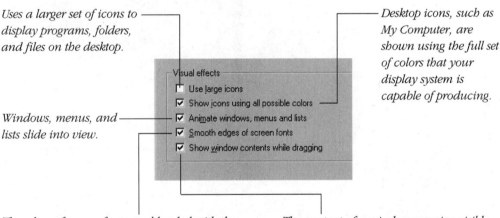

Desktop icons, such as My Computer, are shown using the full set of colors that your display system is capable of producing.

The edges of screen fonts are blended with the desktop so they appear smoother.

The content of a window remains visible as you move a window by dragging it. Otherwise, only the frame moves while you drag.

About Modifying the Start Menu

To make it easy for you to reorganize the programs on the Start menu, Windows 98 lets you drag folders and shortcuts from submenu to submenu right on the Start menu.

If you want even more control of the Start menu, you can use the Windows Explorer to modify the Start menu. The Start menu's contents are stored within the Start menu folder on your disk. By dragging the icons in the Start menu folder, you can change the corresponding structure of the Start menu. **(Figures 17–18)**

Figure 17. *The contents of the Start menu folder.*

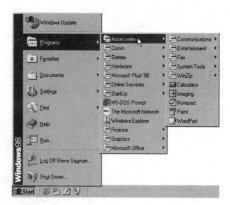

Figure 18. *The corresponding Start menu.*

Figure 19. *Choose Taskbar & Start Menu from the Settings submenu.*

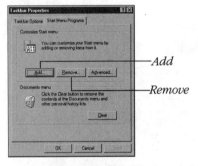

Add
Remove

Figure 20. *Click Add or Remove on the Start Menu Programs tab.*

Figure 21. *The Create Shortcut wizard.*

Figure 22. *Select a folder or icon to remove and then click the Remove button.*

Adding or Deleting Programs on the Start Menu

Installing a new program usually adds a shortcut to the Start menu automatically, but you may need to add a program manually if you obtain a program file, perhaps a small utility program, that does not include an installation program.

1. Click the Start button, choose Settings, and then choose Taskbar & Start Menu from the Settings submenu. **(Figure 19)**

   or

   Click the Taskbar with the right mouse button and choose Properties from the shortcut menu.

2. On the Start Menu Programs tab of the Taskbar Properties dialog box, click Add or Remove. **(Figure 20)**

3. If you are adding a program, follow the steps of the Create Shortcut Wizard which guides you step-by-step through the process. **(Figure 21)**

   or

   If you are deleting a program, open the folder in the Remove Shortcuts/ Folders dialog box that contains the program, select the program, and then click the Remove button. **(Figure 22)**

✔ Tip

■ To remove a Start menu item, you can also click it with the right-mouse button and then choose Delete from the shortcut menu or drag the Start menu item from the Start menu to the Recycle Bin.

Adding/Deleting Start Menu Programs

Reorganizing the Start Menu by Dragging

The easiest way to reorganize Start menu folders and shortcuts is to drag them from submenu to submenu.

1. Open the Start menu and open the submenu that contains the item you want to move. **(Figure 23)**

2. Place the mouse pointer on the item, and press and hold down the mouse button.

3. With the mouse button held down, move the mouse pointer to the submenu to which you'd like to move the item. **(Figure 24)**

4. Move the mouse pointer on the submenu until the black, horizontal bar is in position.

5. Release the mouse button to drop the item into position. **(Figure 25)**

✔ Tip

■ You can drag shortcuts from the Start menu directly to the Quick Launch toolbar on the Taskbar or to the Window desktop. This gives you handy icons you can click to quickly open programs. **(Figure 26)**

Figure 23. *Open the Start menu.*

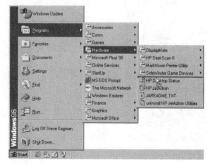

Figure 24. *Hold the mouse button down as you move through the menus.*

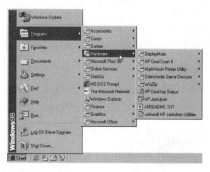

Figure 25. *Release the mouse button to drop the item into position.*

Quick Launch toolbar

Figure 26. *The Quick Launch toolbar.*

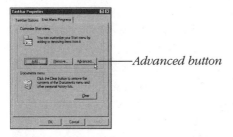

—*Advanced button*

Figure 27. *Click the Advanced button.*

Figure 28. *The Start menu structure appears in the Explorer.*

Figure 29. *Drag an icon to another folder.*

Figure 30. *The Microsoft Plus folder has been moved into the Accessories folder.*

Reorganizing the Start Menu in the Explorer

You can organize the entries on your Start menu into groupings such as Graphics (all your graphics programs and utilities) and Finance (your checkbook or accounting programs).

1. Click the Taskbar with the right mouse button and choose Properties from the shortcut menu.

2. On the Start Menu Programs tab of the Taskbar Properties dialog box, click Advanced. **(Figure 27)** The structure of folders and subfolders that make up the Start menu appears in the Explorer. **(Figure 28)**

3. In the Explorer, open a folder and then drag the icon of the program you want to another folder.

or

Move an entire folder of programs to another folder by dragging it. **(Figures 29–30)**

✔ Tip

■ To add a new group, create a new folder by right-clicking in the Contents pane of the Explorer and then choosing New from the shortcut menu and Folder from the submenu.

Reorganizing the Start Menu

Customizing the Taskbar

You can move the Taskbar to any of the four edges of the screen. You can also change its size and set it to automatically hide when you don't need it.

1. Place the mouse pointer anywhere on the Taskbar. **(Figure 31)**

2. Press and hold the mouse button and drag the Taskbar to the left, right, or top edges of the screen.

3. Release the mouse button to drop the Taskbar at its new location. **(Figure 32)**

✔ Tips

■ To enlarge the Taskbar so it can hold more buttons, drag the inside edge of the Taskbar toward the center of the screen.

■ To hide the Taskbar, click the Taskbar with the right mouse button, choose Properties from the shortcut menu, and then, on the Taskbar Options tab of the Taskbar Properties dialog box, choose Auto hide. The Taskbar will now appear only when you bump the mouse pointer against the edge of the screen where the Taskbar is hiding. **(Figure 33)**

Mouse pointer

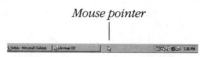

Figure 31. *Place the mouse pointer on the Taskbar.*

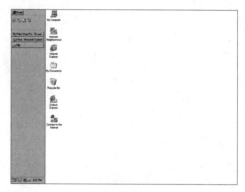

Figure 32. *Drag the Taskbar to another edge of the screen.*

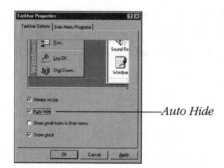

—*Auto Hide*

Figure 33. *Click Auto Hide on the Taskbar properties dialog box to hide the Taskbar until you need it.*

Figure 34. *Double-click the Control panel icon.*

Figure 35. *Double-click the Fonts icon.*

Viewing a Font

1. On the Windows desktop, double-click the My Computer icon.
2. In the My Computer window, double-click the Control Panel icon. **(Figure 34)**
3. In the Control Panel window, double-click the Fonts icon. **(Figure 35)**
4. In the Fonts window, double-click any font to view. **(Figure 36)**
5. Click Done after you view the font. **(Figure 37)**

✔ Tips

■ While you are viewing a font, click the Print button to print a font sample.

■ To see only the main font types without the variations (bold, italic, etc.) choose Hide Variations from the View menu.

■ To see the similarity of other fonts to a particular font, choose List Fonts by Similarity from the View menu. If you move a document to another computer that does not have the same font installed, Windows will substitute a similar font.

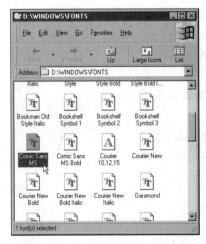

Figure 36. *Double-click the icon for the font to view.*

Figure 37. *The font you've chosen to view.*

Viewing a Font

Adding or Removing a Font

1. On the Windows desktop, double-click the My Computer icon.

2. In the My Computer window, double-click the Control Panel icon.

3. In the Control Panel window, double-click the Fonts icon. **(Figure 38)**

4. From the File menu of the Fonts dialog box, choose Install New Font. **(Figure 39)**

5. In the Add Fonts dialog box, specify the drive and folder that contains the font.

6. On the list of fonts in the Add Fonts dialog box, click the font names of the fonts to add. **(Figure 40)**

7. Click OK.

✔ Tips

■ On the Add Fonts dialog box, make sure Copy Fonts to Windows folder is checked so the font will be copied to the Fonts folder in the Windows folder.

■ To delete a font, select it in the Fonts dialog box and then press the Delete key on the keyboard.

■ Do not remove any of the system fonts (the fonts with the letter "A" in their icon).

Figure 38. *Double-click the Fonts icon.*

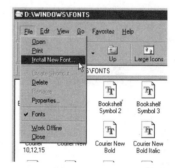

Figure 39. *From the File menu, choose Install New Font.*

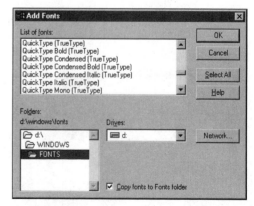

Figure 40. *Select a font from the font list and click OK.*

Figure 41. *Double-click the Mouse icon.*

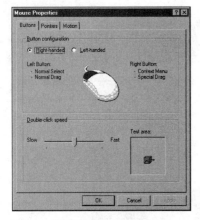

Figure 42. *The Buttons tab.*

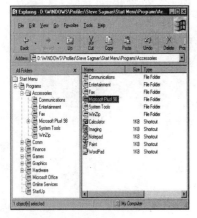

Figure 43. *The Pointers tab.*

Changing Mouse Settings

1. On the Windows desktop, double-click the My Computer icon.

2. In the My Computer window, double-click the Control Panel icon.

3. In the Control Panel window, double-click the Mouse icon. **(Figure 41)**

4. On the tabs of the Mouse Properties dialog box, choose the settings you want. **(Figures 42–44)**

5. Click Apply to see the change immediately or click OK to accept the change and close the Mouse Properties dialog box.

✔ Tip

■ On the Pointers tab of the Mouse Properties dialog box, you can choose a preset scheme from the Schemes drop-down list. **(Figure 43)**

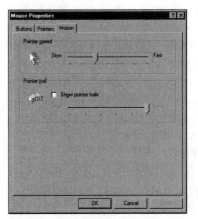

Figure 44. *The Motion tab.*

Changing Mouse Settings

Changing Sound Settings

If your computer has sound capabilities, you can assign sounds to system events, such as a window opening or closing. You can also choose one of the preset sound schemes that comes with Windows.

1. On the Windows desktop, double-click the My Computer icon.

2. In the My Computer window, double-click the Control Panel icon.

3. In the Control Panel window, double-click the Sounds icon. **(Figure 45)**

4. To assign a sound to a system event, click the event on the Events list in the Sounds Properties dialog box and then choose a sound from the Sound Name drop-down list. **(Figure 46)**

5. Click Apply to try out the new sounds or click Close to accept all the sounds and close the Sounds Properties dialog box.

✔ **Tips**

■ To preview a sound, choose the sound from the Sounds Name drop down list and click the right arrow button next to Preview.

■ To save the new scheme of sounds you've created, click the Save As button and then enter a name for the scheme in the Save Scheme As dialog box. **(Figure 47)**

■ You can choose one of the preset sound schemes on the Schemes drop-down list.

Figure 45. *Double-click the Sounds icon.*

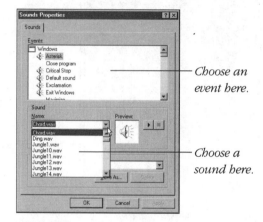

Figure 46. *Choose a sound to associate with the event selected on the Events list.*

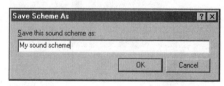

Figure 47. *Name a sound scheme to save it.*

MaintainingYourComputer 7

In this Chapter...

You will learn to perform tasks, some only occasional and some routine, that will help to keep your system in good running order.

To protect your data, you'll want to conduct periodic backups of the files on your hard disk. The Windows Backup program lets you save folders and files on diskettes, a tape backup drive, or on another hard disk in your system.

To keep your hard disk working well, Windows 98 includes several utilities that can remove unused files, detect and repair disk errors, and defragment your disks so their files are stored neatly and efficiently.

The Maintenance Wizard, new to Windows 98, lets you schedule maintenance tasks at night or while you are away from the office, and the new Windows Update utility scans your system, connects to the Microsoft Web site, and downloads any new system components or updates that have become available.

Changing the Date and Time

The clock on the Taskbar displays the current time. If you place the pointer on the clock and pause for a moment the current date appears. **(Figure 1)**

1. Double-click the clock on the Taskbar. **(Figure 1)**

2. In the Date/Time Properties dialog box, set the current date and time using the controls. **(Figure 2)**

3. Click OK.

✔ Tips

- If you don't see the clock on your Taskbar, you can turn on the clock by clicking the Start button, choosing Settings, and then choosing Taskbar & Start Menu. Turn on the Show clock option on the Taskbar Properties dialog box. **(Figure 3)**

- If you are moving from place to place with a portable computer, the Time Zone tab of the Date/Time Properties dialog box lets you change the current time zone.

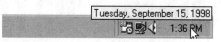

Figure 1. *Double-click the clock.*

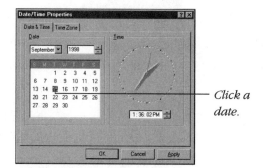

Figure 2. *Set the current date and time.*

Click a date.

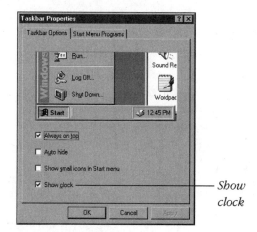

Show clock

Figure 3. *Click Show clock to make the clock visible.*

Changing the Date and Time

Figure 4. *The first screen of the wizard.*

Figure 5. *Choose Back up My Computer.*

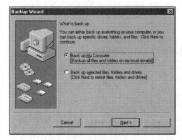

Figure 6. *Choose whether to back up all files or only those that are new or changed.*

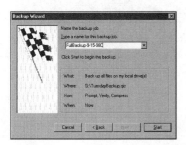

Figure 7. *Enter a name for the backup job.*

Backing Up Your Entire Hard Disk

Using the Backup system tool, you can create a safe copy of some or all of the information on your hard disk. You can back up your data to a tape drive, to floppy disks, or to another drive on your system or on the network.

1. Open the Start menu, and then the Accessories submenu.

2. From the Accessories submenu, choose System Tools, and then choose Backup from the System Tools submenu. Microsoft Backup opens and displays the first screen of the Backup wizard. **(Figure 4)**

3. Choose Create a New Backup Job and click OK.

4. On the next screen, choose Back Up My Computer and click Next. **(Figure 5)**

5. On the next screen, choose All selected files or choose New and changed files to back up only files that are new or that have changed since the last time you backed up your system, and click Next. **(Figure 6)**

7. Choose a back up destination and click Next.

8. Choose whether to compare the backup with the original files and whether to compress the backed up data, and then click Next.

9. Enter a name for the backup job, and then click Next. **(Figure 7)** All backup files are stored in a single compressed file with a QIC extension.

Backing Up Your Entire Hard Disk

Conducting a Partial Backup

After you have done a full system backup, you may want to do periodic backups of certain files or folders, or of all files that have changed since the last backup.

1. On the first screen of the Backup wizard, choose Back Up Selected Files, Folders, and Disks, and click Next.

2. In the left pane, double-click the icon for the disk that you want to back up. The list in the right pane displays the folders on that drive. **(Figure 8)**

   To select all files in a folder, click the check box in front of the folder name. **(Figure 9)**

   To select some of the files in a folder, double-click the folder name and then click the check box in front of each file that you want to back up. **(Figure 10)**

3. Click Next and continue with the backup procedure. *See previous page.*

✔ Tips

- A backup job stores the list of files and folders to be backed up. Once you have defined a backup job, you can simply open the job whenever you want to back up your files—you don't need to select the files each time.

- If you accidentally check a file or folder, click the check box again to uncheck it.

- After you become familiar with the Backup accessory, you can close the Backup wizard and make all your choices on the Backup tab of the Microsoft Backup program.

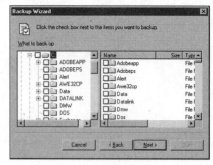

Figure 8. *Double-click an icon to show its contents in the right window.*

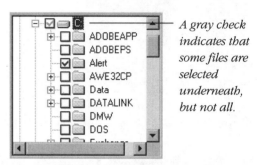

A gray check indicates that some files are selected underneath, but not all.

Figure 9. *Click a check box to select a folder.*

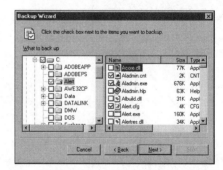

Figure 10. *Click check boxes in the right pane to select individual files for backup.*

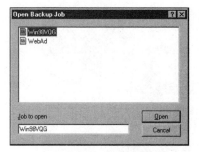

Figure 11. *Select a backup job.*

Name of backup job

What   *Where*   *How*

Figure 12. *The Backup tab.*

Backup Wizard button.

Figure 13. *The Backup Wizard button.*

Using a Backup Job

If you have a group of files that you want to back up on a regular basis, you can save time by using a backup job. A backup job stores the list of files and folders to be backed up. Once you have defined a backup job, you can simply open the job whenever you want to back up your files—you don't need to select the files each time.

1. Open the Backup accessory, and select Open an Existing Backup Job from the first screen of the Backup wizard, and then click OK.

2. Choose the backup job from the list of backup jobs that appears. **(Figure 11)**

The settings stored in the backup job (the files to be backed up, the destination, and the backup job's name) appear on the Backup tab of the Microsoft Backup program. **(Figure 12)**

2. Check the settings on the Backup tab, and then click Start.

3. When prompted whether to overwrite the existing backup job, click OK.

✔ Tip

■ To return to the Backup wizard, which will take you through the process of creating a new backup job step by step, click the Backup Wizard button on the toolbar. **(Figure 13)**

Using a Backup Job

Restoring Backed Up Files

You must use the Backup program to restore files that you have backed up.

1. Open the Backup accessory.

2. Choose Restore backed up files on the first screen of the Backup wizard, and click OK. **(Figure 14)**

3. On the Restore From screen, select the backup job that you want to restore and click Next. **(Figure 15)**

4. On the next screen of the wizard, check to make sure the backed up information that you want to restore is checked, and then click OK. **(Figure 16)**

✔ **Tip**

■ To adjust the restore options, click Cancel on the wizard and then make settings changes on the Restore tab of the Microsoft Backup program. **(Figure 17)**

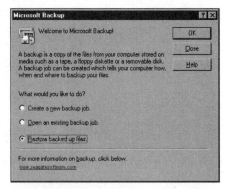

Figure 14. *Click Restore backed up files.*

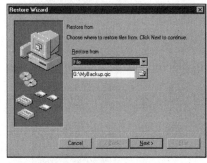

Figure 15. *Select the backup job to restore.*

Figure 16. *Confirm that the backup set is correct and click OK.*

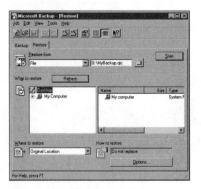

Figure 17. *The Restore tab.*

Figure 18. *Select Disk Cleanup from the System Tools submenu.*

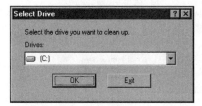

Figure 19. *Select a drive.*

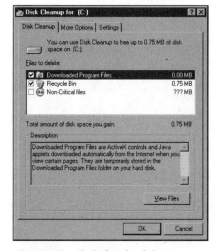

Figure 20. *Click the check boxes next to the items you want to delete.*

Cleaning Up a Disk

The new Disk Cleanup program in Windows 98 can scan your disks and help to remove files that are extraneous, such as old temporary files and downloaded Internet pages. Before it removes files, it shows you what it thinks should be deleted, so you can contradict its selections, if necessary.

1. From the Start menu, choose Programs, and then choose Accessories.

2. From the Accessories submenu, choose System Tools, and then choose Disk Cleanup. **(Figure 18)**

3. Select the drive to be cleaned up and then click OK. **(Figure 19)** The Disk Cleanup program scans the disk and locates files that it thinks can be deleted.

4. Make sure the check boxes next to the files you want to delete are checked and then click OK. **(Figure 20)**

✔ Tips

■ You can click View Files to see files before you delete them.

■ The More Options tab of the Disk Cleanup program offers more ways you can regain disk space.

Compressing a Disk

A hard disk is like a closet. It's always nearly full, no matter how large it is. Rather than buy a bigger hard disk, you can use the DriveSpace system tool to create a compressed drive. This gives you about double the storage capacity at the slight expense of some speed saving and retrieving files.

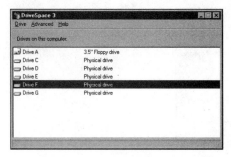

Figure 21. *Select a drive to compress.*

1. From the Accessories submenu of the Start menu, choose System Tools.

2. From the System Tools submenu, choose DriveSpace.

3. Select the drive that you want to compress. **(Figure 21)**

4. From the Drive menu, choose Compress. DriveSpace will show you the change in free space that it will create.

5. Click Start to proceed. **(Figure 22)**

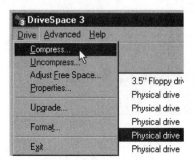

Figure 22. *Choose Compress from the File menu.*

✔ Tips

■ Because DriveSpace has to compress and uncompress files as you use them, you may notice a slight delay when opening and saving files on the compressed drive. Therefore, it's better to place data rather than program files on the compressed drive.

■ Creating a compressed drive is a slow process. You might want to compress a drive overnight or when you leave the office.

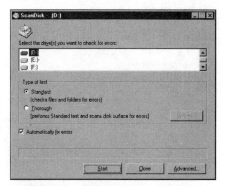

Figure 23. *Select a drive to check.*

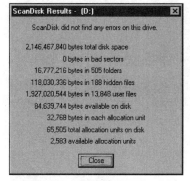

Figure 24. *The test results in summary form.*

Detecting and Repairing Disk Errors

The ScanDisk accessory checks your drives for errors and fixes them.

1. From the Accessories submenu, choose System Tools.
2. From the System Tools submenu, choose ScanDisk.
3. Select the drive that you want to scan. **(Figure 23)**
4. Select the type of test: Standard or Thorough.
5. If you want ScanDisk to automatically fix errors without prompting you, turn on the Automatically Fix Errors option.
6. Click Start.
7. Answer any screen prompts regarding disk errors.

When the scan is complete, you will see a summary of the test. **(Figure 24)** You can then close any open Scandisk dialog boxes.

✔ Tips

■ To optimize disk performance and capacity on your drives, you should conduct the Standard test every week or two.

■ Allow at least a half hour to conduct the Thorough scan.

Detecting and Repairing Disk Errors

Defragmenting Your Hard Disk

The Disk Defragmenter system tool rearranges files so that each file is in one contiguous block on the hard disk. It also consolidates all the free space in one location on your disk. After running the defragmenter, you should notice a speed improvement when you start applications, and open and save files.

1. From the Accessories submenu of the Start menu, choose System Tools.

2. On the System Tools submenu, choose Disk Defragmenter.

3. In the Select Drive dialog box, choose the drive that you want to defragment and click OK. **(Figure 25)**

✔ Tips

■ Defragmenting a drive can take a long time (30–90 minutes). You can begin the process before a lunch break or you can multitask and switch to another application.

■ If you want to get a visual representation of the defragmenting process, click Show Details in the Defragmenting Drive dialog box. Then click Legend to interpret what each colored box means. **(Figure 26)**

■ You can use the Maintenance Wizard, also on the System Tools submenu, to schedule disk defragmenting so that it occurs overnight.

Figure 25. *Choose a drive to defragment.*

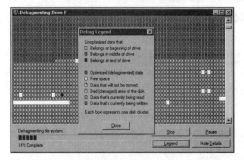

Figure 26. *Click Legend to open a guide to the colors and symbols in the Details display.*

Defragmenting Your Hard Disk

Figure 27. Click a floppy drive with the right mouse button and choose Format from the shortcut menu.

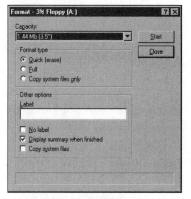

Figure 28. Choose a disk capacity and format type.

Formatting a Diskette

Unless you buy preformatted floppy disks, you will need to format diskettes before using them.

1. Double-click the My Computer icon on the desktop.

2. Click the icon for the floppy drive with the right mouse button.

3. From the shortcut menu, choose Format. **(Figure 27)**

4. Choose the capacity of the disk and the format type. **(Figure 28)**

5. Click Start.

6. When formatting is complete, study the contents of the Format Results dialog box, and click Close.

7. To format other floppy disks, repeat steps 4–6.

8. Close the Format dialog box when you are finished formatting.

✔ Tips

- A fast way to remove all the files from a floppy disk is to choose Quick rather than Full format.

- Be sure to single, not double-click, the floppy drive icon in My Computer. If you double-click, the Format option will not appear on the File menu. If you do this accidentally, click the Up icon on the toolbar, and try again.

Formatting a Diskette

Emptying the Recycle Bin

All files, folders, and shortcuts that you delete go into the Recycle Bin. Space on your hard drive is not freed up until you tell Windows to empty the Recycle Bin.

1. Double-click the Recycle Bin icon on the desktop. **(Figure 29)**

2. Scroll through the folder to make sure there aren't any files you want to keep. **(Figure 30)**

3. If it's visible, you can click the "Empty Recycle Bin" link in the Recycle Bin window. **(Figure 30)**

or

Choose Empty Recycle Bin from the File menu.

4. Choose Yes to confirm. **(Figure 31)**

✔ Tips

■ If you find any files in the Recycle Bin that you want to keep, click them with the right mouse button and choose Restore from the shortcut menu.

■ If you have any applications open, you may need to minimize them to get to the Recycle Bin icon on the desktop.

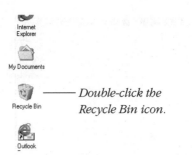

Double-click the Recycle Bin icon.

Figure 29. *Double-click the Recycle Bin icon.*

Empty Recycle Bin link

Figure 30. *Click the Empty Recycle Bin link.*

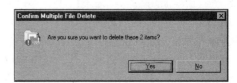

Figure 31. *Click Yes to confirm deletion of the Recycle Bin items.*

Emptying the Recycle Bin

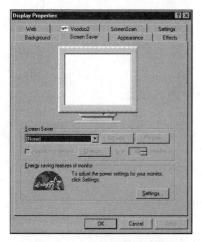

Figure 32. *The Screen Saver tab.*

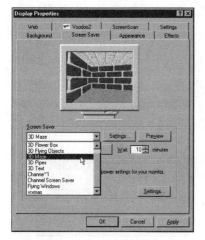

Figure 33. *Select a Screen Saver from the list.*

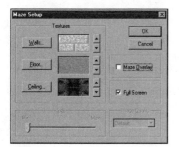

Figure 34. *The settings for the 3-D Maze screen saver.*

Setting Up a Screen Saver

Windows 98 comes with screen savers that can start after your machine is idle for a set length of time.

1. Click the Windows desktop with the right mouse button, and then choose Properties from the shortcut menu.

2. Click the Screen Saver tab of the Display Properties dialog box. **(Figure 32)**

5. Select a screen saver from the list. **(Figure 33)**

6. Click OK.

✔ Tips

■ The screen saver activates after you haven't used the keyboard or mouse for a preset time. To change this delay, enter a larger number in the Wait field.

■ To change screen saver settings, click the Settings button on the Display Properties dialog box. Each screen saver has different settings. **(Figure 34)**

Setting Up a Screen Saver

Changing Your Computer's Password

1. Click the Start button, and choose Settings.

2. From the Settings submenu, choose Control Panel.

3. Double-click the Passwords icon in the Control Panel folder. **(Figure 35)**

4. In the Passwords Properties dialog box, click Change Windows Password. **(Figure 36)**

5. Enter your old and new passwords. **(Figure 37)**

6. Click OK to close the Change Windows Password dialog box.

7. Click OK to close the Passwords Properties dialog box.

✔ Tips

■ Keep your password simple; if you forget it, you won't be able to get into a network to which you are connected.

■ If security is not an issue for you, you don't have to have a password. By leaving the New password and Confirm new password fields blank, you will not need to enter a password when you log on.

Figure 35. *Double-click the Passwords icon.*

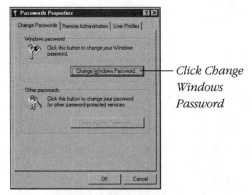

Figure 36. *Click Change Windows Password.*

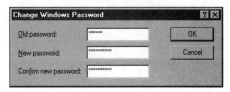

Figure 37. *Enter both the old and new passwords.*

Changing Your Computer's Password

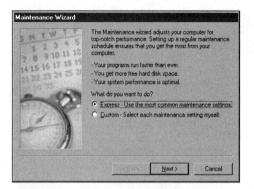

Figure 38. *The first screen of the Maintenance Wizard.*

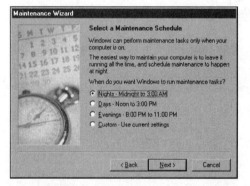

Figure 39. *Select a maintenance schedule.*

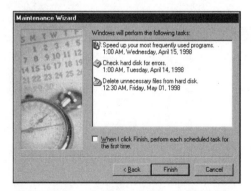

Figure 40. *The tasks that the wizard will perform.*

Running the Maintenance Wizard

The Maintenance Wizard, a new feature of Windows 98, can run maintenance programs according to a schedule you set. This enables you to run programs like the Disk Defragmenter and Disk Cleanup at night, while you are sleeping.

1. From the Accessories submenu of the Start menu, choose System Tools.

2. On the System Tools submenu, choose Maintenance Wizard.

3. On the first screen of the wizard, click Express to use common settings or click Custom to choose your own settings. **(Figure 38)**

4. If you choose Express, the wizard will ask for the time at which you want to run maintenance tasks. **(Figure 39)** If you choose Custom, the wizard will show you each maintenance task and ask you to select options.

5. Click Finish on the last screen of the wizard to start the wizard. **(Figure 40)** Your maintenance tasks will occur according to the schedule you have set.

✔ Tip

■ To run the maintenance tasks immediately for the first time, click the following option on the last screen of the wizard: When I Click Finish, Perform Each Scheduled Task for the First Time.

Running the Maintenance Wizard

Running Windows Update

If you have an Internet connection, you can run the new Windows Update program. Window Update scans your system, connects to the Microsoft Windows Update Web site, and obtains a list of Windows components that have been updated. The updates you choose from this list will be downloaded and installed automatically.

1. From the Start menu, choose Windows Update. Internet Explorer opens and connects to the Windows Update Web site. **(Figure 41)**

2. Click the Product Updates link. **(Figure 41)**

3. Click the Check box next to each update that you want to install. **(Figure 42)**

4. Click Start Download.

✔ Tip

■ After you update Windows components, you can click the Device Driver and System Files section at the bottom of the Update Wizard page to update hardware drivers, such as video or printer drivers.

Figure 41. *The Windows Update Web page at the Microsoft Web site.*

Figure 42. *The Product Updates Web page.*

Adding Hardware and Software

In this Chapter...

You will learn to make basic configuration changes to the hardware and software in your system.

With its built in "plug and play," Window will recognize most new hardware devices that you add and install the appropriate software drivers automatically. But in some cases, you'll need to inform Windows that you've made a change to the system by using the Add New Hardware program.

Windows automatically keeps track of the software you install, too. To remove a program that you no longer use, you can use the special Add/Remove Programs utility in the Windows Control Panel.

Installing a Program

Windows can help you install new programs.

1. Insert the Setup diskette or CD-ROM of the program.

2. Double-click the My Computer icon.

3. In the My Computer window, double-click the Control Panel icon.

4. In the Control Panel window, double-click the Add/Remove Programs icon. **(Figure 1)**

5. On the Install/Uninstall tab of the Add/Remove Programs Properties dialog box, click Install. **(Figure 2)**

6. On the Install Program From Floppy Disk or CD-ROM dialog box, click Next. **(Figure 3)**

7. When the Install Wizard finds the Setup program, click Next to begin the program's install process.

✔ Tip

■ When you start the Install Program wizard, the wizard will automatically search your A: disk and CD-ROM disk for a SETUP program.

Figure 1. *Double-click the Add/Remove Programs icon.*

Figure 2. *Click the Install button.*

Figure 3. *Click Next.*

Installing a Program

Figure 4. *Double-click the Add/Remove Programs icon.*

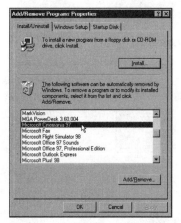

Figure 5. *Select the programs to remove and then click Add/Remove.*

Removing a Program

1. Double-click the My Computer icon.

2. In the My Computer window, double-click the Control Panel icon.

3. In the Control Panel window, double-click the Add/Remove Programs icon. **(Figure 4)**

4. On the Install/Uninstall tab of the Add/Remove Programs Properties dialog box, select the program to remove from the list of programs installed on your system. **(Figure 5)**

5. Click Add/Remove.

✔ Tip

■ To uninstall programs that you installed before you installed Windows 98, you must follow the manufacturer's instructions or run the uninstall program that comes with the software.

Removing a Program

Installing Windows Components

If you do not add all of the available Windows components when you first install Windows 98, you can always add and remove components later.

1. Double-click the My Computer icon.

2. In the My Computer window, double-click the Control Panel icon.

3. In the Control Panel window, double-click the Add/Remove Programs icon. **(Figure 6)**

4. On the Windows Setup tab of the Add/Remove Programs Properties dialog box, click the check box next to a component to install. **(Figure 7)**

5. Double-click the component or click the component and then click the Details button to see the subcomponents of the components. **(Figure 8)**

6. Click the check boxes next to the subcomponents that you want installed.

7. Click OK to close the subcomponents dialog box.

8. Click OK again to begin installing the components you've selected.

✔ Tips

■ Clearing the check in the check box next to a component will remove the component from your system.

■ A gray check box next to a component on the list indicates that only some of the subcomponents will be installed unless you choose otherwise. **(Figure 7)**

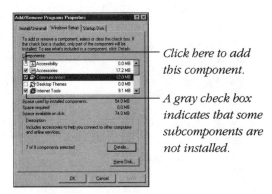

Figure 6. *Double-click the Add/Remove programs icon.*

Click here to add this component.

A gray check box indicates that some subcomponents are not installed.

Figure 7. *Click the check box next to each component to install.*

Figure 8. *Choose subcomponents on the Details dialog box.*

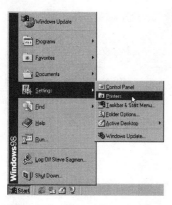

Figure 9. *Choose Printers from the Settings submenu.*

Figure 10. *Double-click the Add Printer icon.*

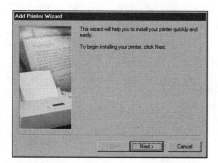

Figure 11. *Follow the steps of the Add Printer Wizard.*

Installing a Printer

You can choose a printer when you first install Windows 98, but if you add a printer to your system, you'll need to install its printer driver.

1. From the Start menu, choose Settings.
2. From the Settings submenu, choose Printers. **(Figure 9)**
3. In the Printers dialog box, double-click the Add Printer icon. **(Figure 10)**
4. Follow the steps of the Add Printer Wizard to select a printer type and printer port. **(Figure 11)**

✔ Tips

- You can also double-click the My Computer icon and then double-click the Printers icon to open the Printers dialog box. **(Figure 12)**
- After you install a printer, an icon for it appears in the Printers dialog box.

Figure 12. *You can also open the Printers dialog box by double-clicking the Printers icon in My Computer.*

Choosing the Default Printer

If you have more than one printer installed, you can set the default printer. The default printer prints your documents unless you specifically choose an alternate printer when you print.

1. Double-click the My Computer icon.

2. In the My Computer window, double-click the Printers icon. **(Figure 13)**

3. Right-click the icon of the printer that you want to use as the default.

4. From the shortcut menu, choose Set as Default. **(Figure 14)**

✔ Tips

■ If you remove the default printer, another printer will be chosen automatically as the default printer.

■ In most programs, you can override the default printer selection when you print a document so you can print to a different printer.

Figure 13. *Double-click the Printers icon.*

Figure 14. *Choose Set as Default from the shortcut menu.*

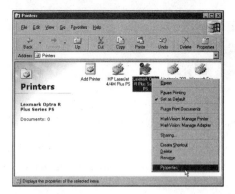

Figure 15. *Choose Properties from the shortcut menu.*

Changing Printer Settings

1. Double-click the My Computer icon.

2. In the My Computer window, double-click the Printers icon.

3. Right-click the icon of the printer whose settings you want to change.

4. From the shortcut menu, choose Properties. **(Figure 15)**

5. On the tabs of the Properties dialog box for the printer, change settings and then click OK. **(Figure 16)**

✔ **Tip**

■ You can test the current printer by choosing Print Test Page on the General tab of the printer Properties dialog box. **(Figure 17)**

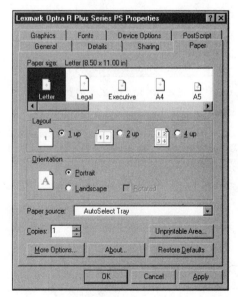

Figure 16. *Change paper settings for the printer on the Paper tab.*

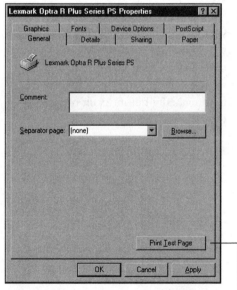

Figure 17. *Click Print Test Page to test your printer.*

Installing a Modem

If a modem is installed in your computer when you install Windows 98, the modem will be detected and set up automatically. If you add a modem later, you must follow this procedure:

1. Double-click the My Computer icon.

2. In the My Computer window, double-click the Control Panel icon.

3. In the Control Panel window, double-click the Modems icon. **(Figure 18)**

4. In the Modems Properties dialog box, click the Add button. **(Figure 19)**

5. Follow the steps of the Install New Modem Wizard to correctly install the new modem into Windows.
(Figure 20)

✔ Tip

■ On the Modems Properties dialog box, you can also set the Dialing properties, which include such settings as the area code from which you are calling, and whether a 9 should be dialed automatically before each number to get an outside line.

Figure 18. *Double-click the Modems icon.*

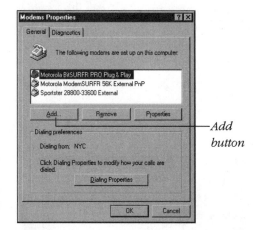

—*Add button*

Figure 19. *Click the Add button to begin installing a new modem.*

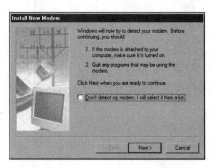

Figure 20. *Follow the steps of the Install New Modem Wizard.*

Installing a Modem

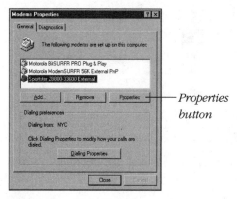

— *Properties button*

Figure 21. *Click the Properties button.*

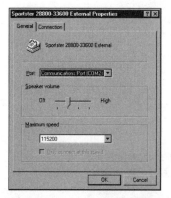

Figure 22. *The General tab.*

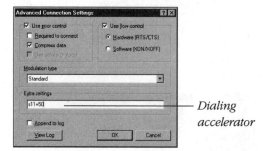

— *Dialing accelerator*

Figure 23. *The Advancd Connection Settings tab.*

Changing Modem Settings

1. Double-click the My Computer icon.

2. In the My Computer window, double-click the Control Panel icon.

3. In the Control Panel window, double-click the Modems icon.

4. In the Modems Properties dialog box, click the Properties button.
(Figure 21)

5. Change settings on the General and Connection tabs of the modem Properties dialog box. **(Figure 22)**

6. Click OK.

✔ Tips

■ To change the really technical settings of your modem, click Advanced on the Connection tab of the modem Properties dialog box.

■ To increase the dialing speed of most modems, click Advanced on the Connection tab of the modem Properties dialog box and then enter S11=50 into the Extra settings box.
(Figure 23)

Changing Modem Settings

Setting Up Other Hardware

Windows can detect most new devices that you add to your system and automatically install the appropriate software for them. If Windows does not automatically recognize a new device, then follow this procedure:

1. Double-click the My Computer icon.

2. In the My Computer window, double-click the Control Panel icon.

3. In the Control Panel window, double-click the Add New Hardware icon. **(Figure 24)**

4. Follow the steps of the Add New Hardware wizard to set up your new device. **(Figures 25–26)**

✔ **Tip**

■ The Add New Hardware will automatically detect any new devices that you've added. If you want, though, you can choose to tell the Wizard which new device you've added by picking from a list. **(Figure 27)**

Figure 24. *Double-click the Add New Hardware icon.*

Figure 25. *Click Next.*

Figure 26. *Follow the steps of the wizard.*

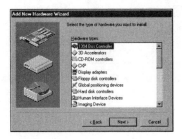

Figure 27. *Choose a device type from the Hardware list.*

Figure 28. *Double-click the Mouse icon.*

Changing the Mouse Settings

1. Double-click the My Computer icon.

2. In the My Computer window, double-click the Control Panel icon.

3. In the Control Panel window, double-click the Mouse icon. **(Figure 28)**

4. Change settings on the tabs of the Mouse Properties dialog box. **(Figures 29–31)**

5. Click OK.

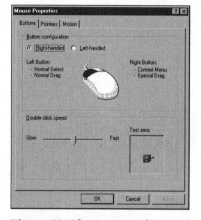

Figure 29. *The Buttons tab.*

Figure 30. *The Pointers tab.*

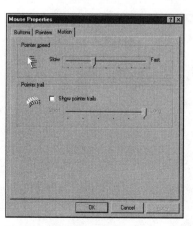

Figure 31. *The Motion tab.*

Changing the Mouse Settings

Setting Up a Computer for Multiple Users

Normally, Windows remembers a single set of preferences and desktop settings. The screen looks the same no matter who logs on. But you can change Windows so that it will remember each user's individual preferences (such as the background wallpaper on the desktop) and restore them the next time that person logs on.

1. Open the Control Panel and double-click the Users icon to open the User Settings dialog box. **(Figure 32)**

2. Click New User to add a new user. **(Figure 33)**

3. Click Next and then enter a new user name when the wizard asks for one and click Next. **(Figure 34)**

4. Enter a password when the wizard asks for one, and click Next. (You can skip this step if you don't want to have to enter a password each time you log in.)

5. Choose the settings that you want Windows to remember and click Next. **(Figure 35)**

6. Click Finish to complete the process.

✔ Tip

■ The two check boxes on the Passwords Properties dialog box allow you to choose which preferences you want to include in each user profile.

Figure 32. *Double-click the users icon.*

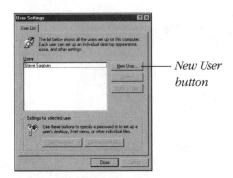

New User button

Figure 33. *Click New User.*

Figure 34. *Enter a new user name.*

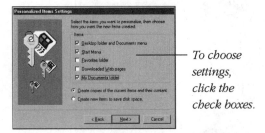

To choose settings, click the check boxes.

Figure 35. *Choose the settings that Windows will maintain for the new user.*

Part 3
Going Online

Part 3
Going Online

Chapter 9: Setting Up a Connection

Chapter 10: Exchanging E-Mail

Chapter 11: Browsing the Internet

Setting Up a Connection

In this Chapter...

You will learn to set up a connection to the Internet with Windows 98.

Browsing the Web has become such an important part of most people's computing experience that Windows 98 incorporates an easy and straightforward procedure for establishing a connection with an Internet Service Provider. One step of the procedure even offers a listing of Internet Service Providers that can provide you with access to the Internet through their dial-up telephone numbers.

Once you have a connection established, you can easily connect to the Internet whenever you want. You can even set your machine to connect to the Internet automatically whenever you enter an Internet address into Windows Explorer, open Internet Explorer, click a Web site link, or try to get your e-mail.

Starting the Internet Connection Wizard

1. Choose Settings from the Start menu, and then choose Control Panel from the Settings submenu.

2. Double-click the Internet icon. **(Figure 1)**

3. On the Connection tab of the Internet Properties dialog box, click the Connect button. **(Figure 2)** The Internet Connection Wizard opens. **(Figure 3)**

✔ Tips

■ The Internet Connection Wizard can help you find an Internet Service Provider (ISP), a local company that provides dial-up phone lines that you can call with your modem to connect to the Internet.

■ You can also start the Wizard by choosing Internet Options from the View menu, and then clicking Connect on the Connection tab of the Internet Options dialog box.

Figure 1. *Double-click the Internet icon.*

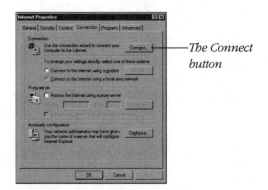

The Connect button

Figure 2. *Click the Connect button.*

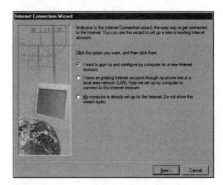

Figure 3. *The first screen of the Internet Connection Wizard.*

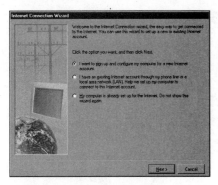

Figure 4. *Choose the first option.*

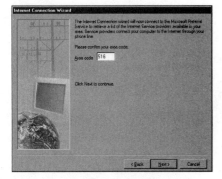

Figure 5. *Enter your area code.*

Figure 6. *Select a modem.*

Signing Up for a New Internet Account

If you do not yet have an Internet account, the Internet Connection Wizard can connect to the Microsoft Referral Service to obtain a list of Internet Service Providers in your area.

1. Open the Internet Connection Wizard. *See "Starting the Internet Connection Wizard" on the previous page.*

2. On the first screen of the wizard, choose "I want to sign up and configure my computer for a new Internet account," and click Next. **(Figure 4)**

3. On the next screen, enter your area code. **(Figure 5)**

4. In the Choose Modem dialog box, select your modem. **(Figure 6)** The wizard will dial the Microsoft Referral Service using a toll-free 800 number.

5. From the list of Internet Service Providers, choose a company with whom you'd like to establish an account and click Next.

6. Following the remaining steps of the wizard to set up a new Internet access account.

✔ Tip

■ After you set up a connection, you can choose Dial-up Networking in the My Computer window and then double-click the icon for the ISP in the Dial-up Networking window to connect to the Internet.

Signing Up for a New Connection

Setting Up an Existing Internet Service

1. Start the Internet Connection Wizard. *See "Starting the Internet Connection Wizard," on page 128.*

2. On the first screen of the Wizard, choose "I have an existing Internet account through my phone line or a local area network (LAN)," and click Next. **(Figures 7–9)**

3. Follow the remaining steps of the wizard.

✔ Tip

■ To change your settings, you can always reopen the Internet Connection Wizard again and follow its steps.

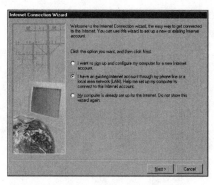

Figure 7. *Choose the second option.*

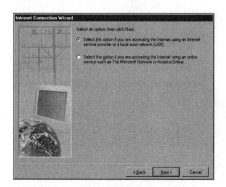

Figure 8. *Select the first option.*

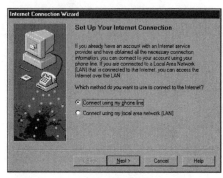

Figure 9. *Continue following the steps of the wizard, clicking Next after each step.*

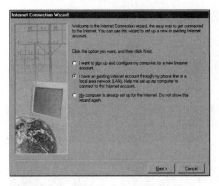

Figure 10. *Choose the second option.*

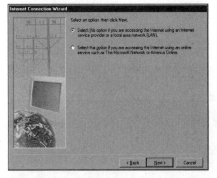

Figure 11. *Leave the first option selected and click Next.*

Figure 12. *Follow the remaining steps of the wizard, clicking Next after each step.*

Connecting to the Internet Through an Office Network

1. Start the Internet Connection Wizard. *See "Starting the Internet Connection Wizard," on page 128.*

2. On the first screen of the Wizard, choose "I have an existing Internet account through my phone line or a local area network (LAN)," and click Next. **(Figure 10)**

3. On the next screen, click Next. **(Figure 11)**

4. On the "Set Up Your Internet Connection" screen, choose Connect Using my Local Area Network (LAN), and click Next. **(Figure 12)**

5. Follow the rest of the steps of the wizard.

✔ Tip

■ The Internet Connection Wizard will ask for information about your proxy server. If your network uses a proxy server, your network administrator can give you the correct entries.

Connecting Through a Network

Setting Windows to Connect Automatically

You can set Windows to open a Dial-Up Connection dialog box each time a program such as Internet Explorer needs to connect to the Internet. You can even have Windows connect to the Internet automatically whenever it's necessary.

1. On the first page of the Internet Connection Wizard, specify that you want to use a phone line or LAN to connect to the Internet, and click Next twice. **(Figure 13)**

2. Specify that you want to connect to the Internet through a phone line rather than a LAN. **(Figure 14)**

3. Follow the remaining steps of the wizard.

✔ Tips

■ To test your connection, open the Internet Explorer. The Dial-up Connection dialog box will open. **(Figure 15)**

■ To have Windows dial the phone automatically without stopping at the Dial-up Connection dialog box, click the Dial Automatically check box. **(Figure 15)**

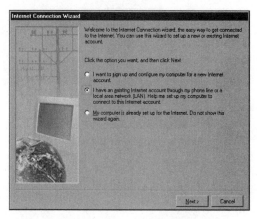

Figure 13. *Choose the second option.*

Figure 14. *Choose the first option.*

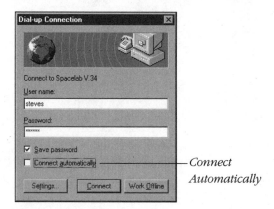

— *Connect Automatically*

Figure 15. *Choose Connect Automatically to have Windows connect without stopping at this dialog box.*

Exchanging E-Mail

In this Chapter...

You will learn to send and receive e-mail with Outlook Express, the e-mail program that is included along with Internet Explorer in Windows 98.

You will learn to open the messages you've received, compose replies, and file away messages in folders within Outlook Express. You will also learn to compose new messages that you will send to individuals or to distribution lists called "groups."

You will also learn to keep an address book of people and groups with whom you correspond. Having an address book available allows you to address a message by entering a recipient's name without having to remember a long and involved e-mail address.

In this Chapter

About Windows 98 E-Mail

Outlook Express, a highly regarded Internet e-mail program, is built right into Windows 98 so you can begin sending and receiving e-mail as soon as you've set up an account with an Internet Service Provider.

Outlook Express provides a filing system that you can use to organize messages and it includes a built-in address book that can hold the e-mail addresses of all the people with whom you correspond.

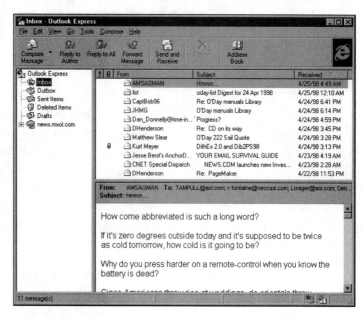

Figure 1. *Outlook Express.*

If you wish, you can also download from the Microsoft Web site a more full-featured e-mail program called Microsoft Outlook. Outlook has the same e-mail handling features of Outlook Express, and it also offers a more advanced address book, a sophisticated calendar and scheduling system, and a handy task list to keep track of your to-do items. If you download Microsoft Outlook, you'll be able to use all the same procedures for handling e-mail that you'll learn in this chapter.

My Documents

Recycle Bin

 ——— *Outlook Express icon*

Outlook
Express

Figure 2. *Double-click the Outlook Express icon.*

Outlook Express icon

Figure 3. *Click the Outlook Express icon on the Quick Launch toolbar.*

Figure 4. *Choose Outlook Express from the Internet Explorer submenu.*

Opening Outlook Express

Double-click the Outlook Express icon on the Windows desktop. **(Figure 2)**

or

Click the Outlook Express icon on the Quick Launch toolbar that is on the Taskbar. **(Figure 3)**

or

From the the Programs submenu on the Start Menu, choose Internet Explorer, and then choose Outlook Express. **(Figure 4)**

Adding a Mail Account

If you used the Internet Connection Wizard to set up your Internet connection, the Wizard helped you set up a Mail account in Outlook Express. But if you did not use the Internet Connection Wizard, you must add a Mail account manually.

1. From the Tools menu, choose Accounts. **(Figure 5)**

2. On the Mail tab of the Internet Accounts dialog box, click Add and then choose Mail from the submenu. **(Figure 6)**

3. Follow the steps of the Internet Connection Wizard, which will ask for all the information it needs to set up a new Mail account for you. **(Figures 7–8)**

✔ Tips

■ The Internet Connection Wizard will ask whether your mail server is a POP3 or IMAP server. It will also ask for the names of the incoming and outgoing mail servers. Your Internet Service Provider can provide this information to you.

■ If you have an e-mail account with another Internet Service Provider or if more than one person will be using Outlook Express to send and receive e-mail, you can repeat the procedure above to set up additional mail accounts.

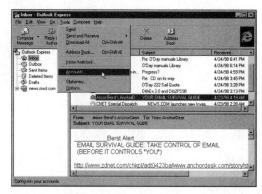

Figure 5. *From the Tools menu, choose Accounts.*

Figure 6. *Click Add and choose Mail.*

Figure 7. *Enter your name.*

Figure 8. *The account you've set up appears on the list of Mail accounts.*

Adding a Mail Account

Send and Receive button.

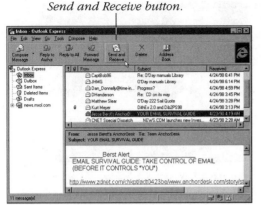

Figure 9. *Click the Send and Receive button.*

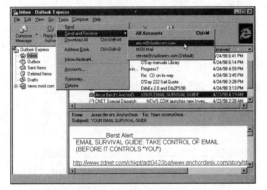

Figure 10. *Choose an account to select from the Send and Receive submenu.*

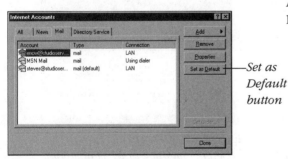

Figure 11. *Click Set as Default.*

Set as
Default
button

Checking for New E-Mail

By default, Outlook Express will check for new e-mail whenever it is started, but you can also check for new e-mail at any time.

1. Click the Send and Receive button on the toolbar. **(Figure 9)**

or

Press Ctrl+M.

✔ Tips

■ If you have set up multiple mail accounts, Outlook Express will check all mail accounts by default. You can check mail for a particular account by choosing Send and Receive from the Tools menu and then choosing the account to check from the Send and Receive submenu. **(Figure 10)**

■ If you have set up multiple mail accounts in Outlook Express, one account is the default. When you compose and send mail messages, the return address of the default mail account will be attached to the message. To change the default mail account, choose Accounts from the Tools menu, select an account on the Accounts tab, and then click the Set as Default button. **(Figure 11)**

Reading a Message

If you have new messages, their entries appear at the top of the list of messages. Unread messages are bold and they are accompanied by an icon that looks like a closed envelope.

1. Make sure the Inbox icon is selected on the list of folders. If it is not selected, click it. **(Figure 12)**

2. Click a bold message header to preview the message in the lower pane.
(Figure 13)

or

Double-click the message header to open the message in its own window.
(Figure 14)

3. After you read the message, you can press Esc or click the Close button at the upper-right corner of the window to close the mesage.

✔ Tip

■ To sort messages, click one of the gray buttons at the tops of the columns, such as From or Received. The messages will be sorted according to that column. To reverse the sort order, click the same button again.

Figure 12. *Select the Inbox.*

Selected   Message
message   preview

Figure 13. *Click a message header to preview the message in the lower pane.*

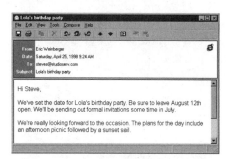

Figure 14. *Double-click a message header to open the message in its own window.*

Reply to Author button

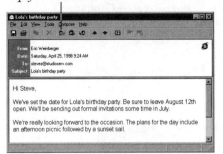

Figure 15. *Click the Reply to Author button within the message.*

Reply to Author button

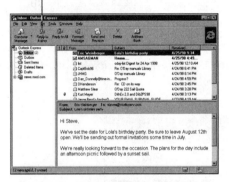

Figure 16. *Click the Reply to Author button on the Outlook Express toolbar.*

Send button.

Figure 17. *Enter your reply above the original message and click Send.*

Replying to a Message

1. Open the message and then click the Reply to Author button on the toolbar within the message window. **(Figure 15)**

or

Click the message header and then click the Reply to Author button on the toolbar. **(Figure 16)**

2. Enter the text of your reply. The text you type will appear above the original message to which you are replying. **(Figure 17)**

3. Click the Send button on the toolbar. The message is moved to the Outbox.

✔ Tips

■ If you are connected to a LAN, your message will be sent immediately.

■ If your Internet Connection is set to dial whenever necessary, Windows will connect to the Internet and then send the message automatically.

■ If the original message to which you are replying was sent to you and other people, you can click Reply to All to send a reply to everyone to whom the original message was addressed.

■ The Subject line of a reply is automatically filled in for you, but you can change it.

Creating a New Message

1. Click Compose Message on the toolbar. **(Figure 18)**

2. Enter the recipient's e-mail address on the "To:" line or click the Select Recipients button to select a recipient from the list. **(Figure 19)**

3. Press Tab to move the cursor to the CC and BCC lines and enter e-mail addresses or names if you want to send copies or blind copies to additional recipients.

4. Press Tab to move the cursor to the Subject line and enter a subject that will be meaningful to the recipient.

5. Press Tab to move the cursor to the message area and type the text of the message.

6. Click Send on the toolbar to send the message. **(Figure 20)**

✔ Tips

■ The message is sent using the return address of the default mail account. To send the message from another account, choose Send Message Using from the File menu, and then choose an account from the submenu. **(Figure 21)**

■ Try to supply a subject that will be meaningful so the recipient will be able to find the filed message later. Avoid using subjects like "Monday AM" or "Various things."

■ If the recipient is in the address book, you can enter just the recipient's name.

■ To send a message to multiple recipients, enter the names or addresses separated by commas or semi-colons.

Compose Message

Figure 18. *Click Compose Message.*

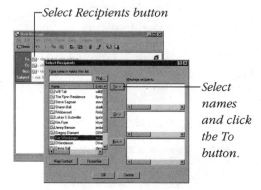

Select Recipients button

Select names and click the To button.

Figure 19. *Click Select Recipients and then select recipients.*

Send button

Figure 20. *Enter the message and click Send.*

Figure 21. *Select an entry from the Send Message Using submenu.*

Select Recipients button

Figure 22. *Click the Select Recipients button.*

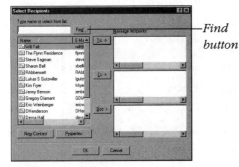

—*Find button*

Figure 23. *Click Find.*

Figure 24. *Choose an online directory.*

Figure 25. *Enter a name and click Find Now.*

Finding an E-Mail Address

If you do not know the e-mail address of the person to whom you want to write, you may be able to look up the address on the Internet.

1. After you click Compose Message, click the Select Recipient button on the "To:" line. **(Figure 22)**

2. In the Select Recipients dialog box, click Find. **(Figure 23)**

3. In the Find People dialog box, choose an online directory from the "Look in" drop-down menu. **(Figure 24)**

4. Enter a name on the Name line, and then click Find Now. **(Figure 25)**

5. When Outlook Express shows you a list of possible e-mail addresses, select the correct address and click the To: CC:, or BCC: buttons to transfer the e-mail address into the message.

✔ Tips

■ You can also click Add to Address Book to add the entry to the Outlook Express address book.

■ The "Look in" drop-down menu lists the major Internet e-mail address directories. If you can't find the e-mail address in one directory, try others.

Finding an E-Mail Address

Forwarding a Message

1. Select a message header in the Inbox and click the Forward Message button on the toolbar. **(Figure 26)**

   or

   Open the message and click the Forward Message button on the toolbar in the message window. **(Figure 27)**

2. Enter the address of the recipient or recipients. **(Figure 28)**

3. If you want, you can tab down to the message text area and enter a note above the original message text.

4. Click Send to send the forwarded message.

✔ Tip

■ The subject line of a forwarded message is preceded by "Fw:" to indicate that the message has been forwarded.

Forward Message button

Figure 26. *Click Forward Message.*

Forward Message button

Figure 27. *Click the Forward Message button within the message.*

Figure 28. *Enter the recipient address.*

Forwarding a Message

Figure 29. *Right-click a folder.*

Figure 30. *Enter a new folder name.*

Click the plus sign.

Figure 31. *Click the plus sign to reveal the sub-folder.*

Figure 32. *The subfolder revealed.*

Filing Messages

Messages that arrive will accumulate in the Inbox unless you delete them or move them to other folders. To organize your e-mail, you can create additional folders that are organized by project, category, sender, or some other scheme.

1. Click any folder in the left pane with the right mouse button and choose New Folder from the shortcut menu. **(Figure 29)**

2. In the Create Folder dialog box, enter a folder name, click a folder on the list, and click OK. **(Figure 30)** The new folder will become a subfolder of the folder you've selected.

3. To reveal the new subfolder, click the plus sign next to the folder above it. **(Figure 31–32)**

4. Click the folder that contains the messages you want to file.

5. Select messages and drag them to the new subfolder.

✔ **Tip**
■ To create a new folder at the main level, right-click the folder named "Outlook Express," and then choose New Folder.

Deleting Messages

1. Select a message to delete. **(Figure 33)**

2. Press the Delete key on the keyboard.

or

Drag the message to the Deleted Items folder. **(Figure 34)**

or

Click the right mouse button and choose Delete from the shortcut menu. **(Figure 35)**

✔ **Tips**

■ To select multiple messages to delete, hold down the Ctrl key as you click each message.

■ To select a sequence of messages to delete, select the first message, hold down the Shift key, and click the last message.

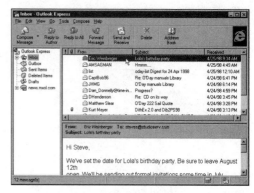

Figure 33. *Select a message to delete.*

Figure 34. *Drag the message to the Deleted Items folder.*

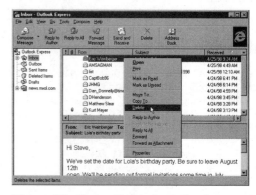

Figure 35. *Choose Delete from the shortcut menu.*

Address Book button

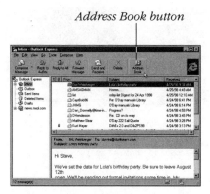

Figure 36. *Click the Address Book button on the toolbar.*

Figure 37. *Click the New Contact button.*

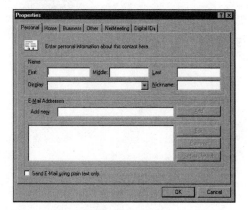

Figure 38. *Enter contact information.*

Adding an Entry to the Address Book

1. Click the Address Book button on the toolbar. **(Figure 36)**

2. Click the New Contact button on the Address Book toolbar. **(Figure 37)**

3. Enter the information you have for the contact onto the tabs of the Properties dialog box. **(Figure 38)**

✔ Tip

■ Outlook Express can maintain multiple e-mail addresses for a contact, one of which is the default. If you enter the contact name into the To: field of a new message, Outlook Express will use the default e-mail address. To change the default, double-click the entry in the Address Book, select an e-mail address, and then click Set as Default.

Adding an Entry to the Address Book

Adding a Sender's Address to the Address Book

1. While a message from a new correspondent is open, right-click the name on the "From:" line.

2. Choose Add to Address Book from the shortcut menu. **(Figure 39)**

✔ Tip

■ To see whether someone who has sent you mail is already in the address book, right-click the name on the "From:" line of a message and choose Find from the shortcut menu. If the name is in the Address Book, it will be found. **(Figure 40)**

Figure 39. *Right-click the From name and choose Add to Address Book from the shortcut menu.*

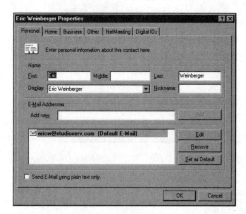

Figure 40. *This name is already in the Address Book.*

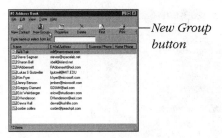

—New Group button

Figure 41. *Click the New Group button.*

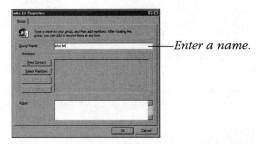

—Enter a name.

Figure 42. *Enter a group name.*

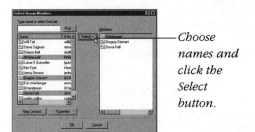

—Choose names and click the Select button.

Figure 43. *Select names and click the Select button.*

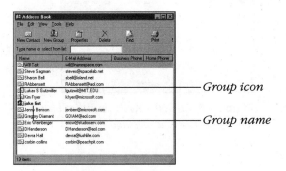

—Group icon

—Group name

Figure 44. *Group names are bold.*

Creating a Distribution List

A "group" in the Address Book is a distribution list that can contain multiple e-mail addresses. By entering the group name on the "To:" line of a new message, you can send the message to everyone in the group.

1. Click the Address Book icon on the toolbar to open the Address Book.

2. Click the New Group button in the Address Book window. **(Figure 41)**

3. Enter a name for the group in the Group Name field. **(Figure 42)**

4. Click the Select Members button. **(Figure 42)**

5. Select names in the Address Book and then click the Select button to add the names to the Members list. **(Figure 43)**

6. Click OK on the Select Group Members dialog box and then click OK on the Properties dialog box. The group name now appears on the list. It's bold and accompanied by a "group" icon. **(Figure 44)**

✔ Tip

- To check the list of members in a group, select the group name in the Address Book and click the Properties button on the toolbar.

Creating a Distribution List

Adding an Automatic Signature

You can have Outlook Express add a line or two of text at the end of each message you send. The text can contain anything you'd like to use to personalize your e-mail, such as your name, company name, phone number, or perhaps even a favorite quote.

1. From the Tools menu, choose Stationery.

2. On the Mail tab of the Stationery dialog box, click Signature. **(Figure 45)**

3. Enter the signature text in the Text field and click OK. **(Figure 46)**

   or

   Click the File button and click Browse to choose a file to use, then click OK.

4. Click OK on the Stationery dialog box.

✔ Tip

■ In the Signature dialog box, you can click the "Add this signature to all outgoing messages" check box. Otherwise, to add a signature to each new message, you must click the Add Signature button on the toolbar when you finish writing the message. **(Figure 47)**

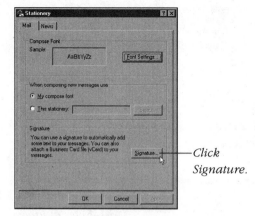

—Click Signature.

Figure 45. *Click Signature.*

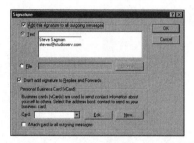

Figure 46. *Enter the signature text.*

Add Signature button

Figure 47. *Click the Add Signature button when you finish a message.*

Insert File button

Figure 48. *Click the Insert File button.*

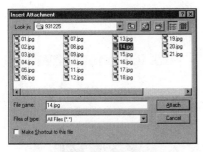

Figure 49. *Select a file to attach.*

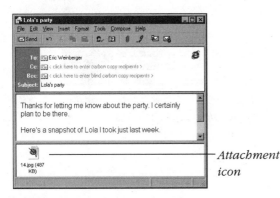

Attachment icon

Figure 50. *Attachments appear in a separate pane.*

Attaching a File

Attaching a file to a message allows you to send a document, scanned photo, or work file along with your e-mail.

1. While you are composing a new message, click the Insert File button on the toolbar. **(Figure 48)**

2. Navigate to the file in the Insert Attachment dialog box and then select the file. **(Figure 49)**

3. Click Attach.

✔ Tips

■ Attachments appear in a separate pane at the bottom of the message window. **(Figure 50)**

■ You can attach more than one file to a message, but don't attach too many or the message may become large and lengthy to send.

■ To remove an attachment, select the attachment's icon, right-click, and then choose Remove from the shortcut menu.

Attaching a File

Receiving an Attachment

When you receive an attachment, an attachment icon appears next to the message on the message list, and the attachment appears below the text of the message within the message. **(Figure 51)** You can save a copy of the attachment on your hard disk so you can work with it.

1. Open the message.
2. Click the attachment with the right mouse button.
3. Choose Save As from the shortcut menu. **(Figure 52)**
4. Navigate to the folder in which you'd like to save the attachment.
5. Change the name, if you'd like.
6. Click Save. **(Figure 53)**

✔ Tips

■ You can also double-click the attachment icon to open the attached file immediately. You may then be able to save the file to your hard disk from within the program that opens the attachment.

■ The original attachment remains in the message so you can always reopen the message to retrieve the original.

■ You may find it easy to save the attachment to the Windows desktop and then move the file into a folder from there.

Attachment icon

Figure 51. *Attachment icon.*

Figure 52. *Right-click the attachment and choose Save As.*

Figure 53. *Select a location for the attachment and click Save.*

Receiving an Attachment

Figure 54. *Choose Rich Text (HTML).*

Insert Picture button

Formatting toolbar

Figure 55. *A Formatting toolbar appears.*

Figure 56. *Sample formatted text.*

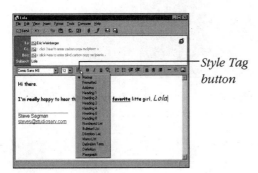

Style Tag button

Figure 57. *Choose a Style Tag from the list to apply a preset format.*

Sending an HTML Message with Pictures and Formatted Text

If you know that the recipient is also using Outlook Express, you can send an e-mail message in HTML format, which can contain pictures and formatted text.

1. Click Compose Message to start a new message.

2. From the Format menu, choose Rich Text (HTML). **(Figure 54)** A Formatting toolbar appears when you move the cursor down into the text area. **(Figure 55)**

3. Enter text, select the text, and then click one of the buttons on the Formatting toolbar to apply your choice of formatting to the text. **(Figure 56)**

4. To insert a picture, position the cursor where you want the picture to appear, and then click the Insert Picture button. **(Figure 54)**

✔ Tip

■ In addition to selecting and formatting the text, you can select the text, click the Style Tag button on the toolbar, and then select one of the preset HTML tags. Each tag applies a different look to the text. **(Figure 57)**

Sending Pictures and Formatting Text

Using Stationery

You can apply stationery, background images and text font choices to any message. The stationery will appear within the message when it's read by another Outlook Express user.

1. From the Compose menu, choose Compose New Message Using.

2. From the submenu, choose one of the stationery types. **(Figure 58)** The background image appears in a new message window. **(Figure 59)**

or

1. Click the down-arrow button next to the Compose Message button on the toolbar and then select a stationery type from the drop-down list. **(Figure 60)**

✔ Tips

■ You can set default stationery for all new messages by choosing Stationery from the Tools menu, clicking This Stationery, and then clicking the Select button to select a stationery type.

■ To remove stationery after you start a message, choose Apply Stationery from the Format menu and then choose No Stationery from the submenu.

Figure 58. *Choose a stationery type.*

Figure 59. *The background image of the stationery appears in the message window.*

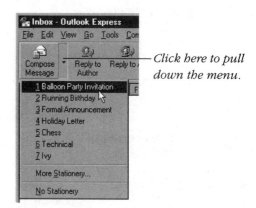

Figure 60. *Choose a stationery from the Compose Message menu.*

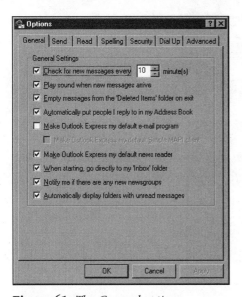

Figure 61. *The General options.*

Changing E-Mail Options

1. From the Tools menu, choose Options.

2. Change settings on the tabs of the Options dialog box. **(Figures 61–63)**

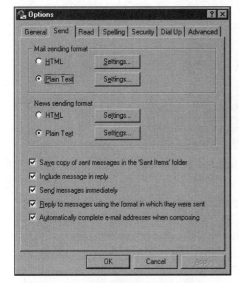

Figure 62. *The Send options.*

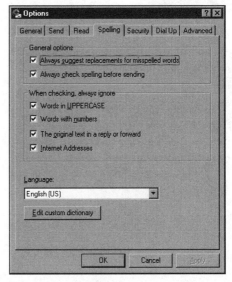

Figure 63. *The Spelling options.*

Using the Inbox Assistant

The Inbox Assistant can process incoming messages for you, sorting messages into folders, deleting unwanted messages, and automatically replying to others.

1. From the Tools menu, choose Inbox Assistant. **(Figure 64)**

2. On the Inbox Assistant dialog box, click Add to add a new rule. **(Figure 65)**

3. Enter criteria into the top half of the Properties dialog box. **(Figure 66)**

4. Choose an action from the bottom half of the Properties dialog box, and click OK. **(Figure 66)**

5. Add another rule or click OK to return to the Inbox Assistant dialog box. **(Figure 67)**

✔ Tips

■ To automatically delete messages, have them moved to the Deleted Items folder.

■ To turn off a rule, open the Inbox Assistant and then clear the check box next to the rule or remove the rule to get rid of it altogether.

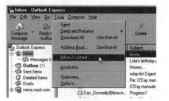

Figure 64. *Choose Inbox Assistant.*

Figure 65. *Click Add.*

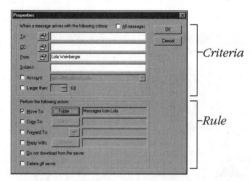

Figure 66. *Enter criteria and an action.*

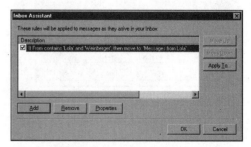

Figure 67. *The new rule appears on the list.*

Using the Inbox Assistant

Browsing the Internet

In this Chapter...

You will learn to browse the Web with Windows 98's Internet Explorer.

Internet Explorer is a Web browser, which reads and displays Web pages at Web sites. Navigating from page to page is particularly easy; you just click on links or buttons on Web pages.

With Internet Explorer, you can also maintain a list of your favorite Web sites, called "Favorites," and place your very favorite Favorites on the Links bar, where they will always be just one click away.

Internet Explorer's integrated searching mechanism lets you find Web pages through the popular, commercial search engines such as Yahoo, Excite, and Infoseek.

In this Chapter

Starting Internet Explorer

Double-click the Internet Explorer icon on the desktop. **(Figure 1)**

or

Click the Internet Explorer icon on the Quick Launch toolbar on the Taskbar. **(Figure 2)**

✔ Tips

■ You can also enter a Web site address, such as www.studioserv.com, into the Address field of any window, such as the My Computer window. The window will convert into an Internet Explorer window, which will take you to the site. **(Figure 3)**

■ Clicking a link in a document also opens Internet Explorer.

■ You can add an Address Bar to the Taskbar by right-clicking the Taskbar and choosing Address from the Toolbars menu. Entering a Web site address into the Address Bar will automatically start Internet Explorer and take you to the site. **(Figures 4–5)**

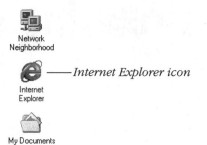

Figure 1. *Double-click the Internet Explorer icon.*

Figure 2. *Click the Internet Explorer icon on the Quick Launch toolbar.*

Figure 3. *Enter an Internet Address into the Address field in any window.*

Figure 4. *Choose Address from the shortcut menu.*

Figure 5. *The Address toolbar on the Taskbar.*

Figure 6. *Click an underlined link.*

Figure 7. *Click a button on a Web page.*

Following Links

Click an underlined link on a Web page to move to a new location on the Web. **(Figure 6)**

or

Click a navigation button on a Web page. **(Figure 7)**

or

Use the controls on the navigation toolbar. **(Figure 8)**

✔ Tip

- To return to the previous page, you can also press the Backspace key on the keyboard.

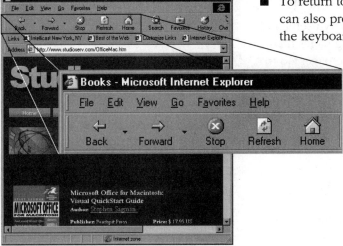

Figure 8. *Click the Back or Forward button to move to the previous or next Web page.*

Going Home

The Home page is the page to which you can always quickly return by clicking the Home button on the toolbar.

Click the Home button on the toolbar. **(Figure 9)**

✔ Tips

■ Your default home page depends on the configuration of your system. Online services and many Internet Service Providers set your home page to their starting page automatically.

■ Excite and Yahoo have very useful and fully customizable starting pages that you can set as your home page. Go to www.yahoo.com or www.excite.com.

Setting Your Home Page

1. Go to the Web page that you'd like to set as your home page.
2. From the View menu, choose Internet Options.
3. On the General tab of the Internet Options dialog box, click Use Current. **(Figure 10)**

✔ Tip

■ Click Use Default to use the standard home page for Internet Explorer, which is at the Microsoft Web site.

Home button

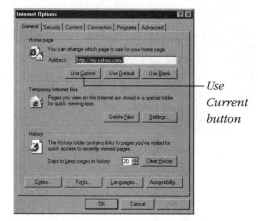

Figure 9. *Click the Home button.*

Use Current button

Figure 10. *Navigate to a favorite page and click Use Current.*

Refresh button

Figure 11. *Click the Refresh button on the toolbar.*

Refreshing a Page

When you visit a Web page, Internet Explorer will pull in the current version, but if a page is frequently updated, it may be updated while you are visiting the site. By refreshing the page, you can pull in the most updated version.

Click the Refresh button on the toolbar. **(Figure 11)**

or
Press F5.

✔ **Tip**

■ If your Internet connection is a little flaky and you are unable to retrieve a page with all its graphics, you can hit Refresh so Internet Explorer can try again.

Going to a Favorite Place

Clicking an entry on the Favorites list allows you to quickly return to a Web site you've designated as a favorite place.

1. Click the Favorites button on the toolbar to open the Favorites Bar. **(Figure 12)**

2. Click a folder on the Favorites Bar to reveal its links. **(Figures 13–14)**

3. Click a link.

or

1. Choose a link from the Favorites menu. **(Figure 15)**

✔ **Tips**

■ You can also choose Favorites from the Start menu to see the Favorites list.

■ You can leave the Favorites Bar visible so you can quickly navigate to all your favorite places.

■ Click the Close button on the Favorites Bar to close the bar.

Favorites button

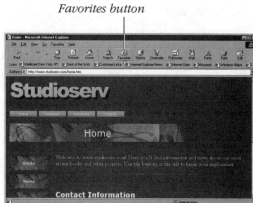

Figure 12. *Click the Favorites button.*

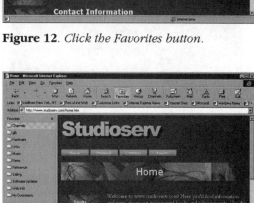

Figure 13. *Click a folder on the Favorites Bar.*

Figure 15. *Choose a link from the Favorites menu.*

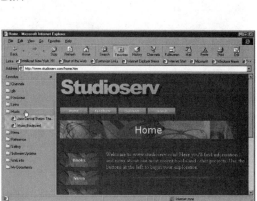

Figure 14. *Click a folder to reveal the links inside.*

Going to a Favorite Place

Figure 16. *Choose Add to Favorites.*

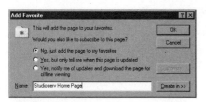

Figure 17. *Leave the first option selected.*

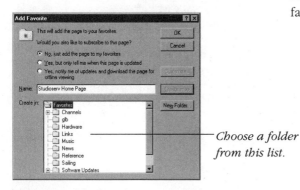

Choose a folder from this list.

Figure 18. *The list of Favorites folders appears when you click the Save In button.*

Storing a Favorite Place

You can save Web site addresses on your Favorites list so you can return to them easily.

1. Navigate to a Web page that you want to designate as a favorite place.

2. From the Favorites menu, choose Add to Favorites. **(Figure 16)**

3. On the Add Favorites dialog box, choose "No, just add the page to my favorites." **(Figure 17)**

4. Edit the name for the favorite, if you want, and click OK.

✔ Tips

- To place the favorite in a particular folder, click Create In, select the folder, and then click OK. **(Figure 18)**

- Click New Folder to create a new folder for the favorite and other favorites of the same type.

Organizing Favorites

1. From the Favorites menu, choose Organize Favorites. **(Figure 19)**

2. In the Organize Favorites dialog box, double-click a folder to open it, if necessary. **(Figure 20)**

3. Select a link and then click Move, Rename, or Delete.

✔ Tip

■ To add a new folder within a folder, open the folder in the Organize Favorites dialog box and then click the New Folder button on the toolbar.

Figure 19. *Choose Organize Favorites.*

Figure 20. *Choose a Favorite and then click Move, Rename or Delete.*

Organizing Favorites

History button

Figure 21. *Click the History button.*

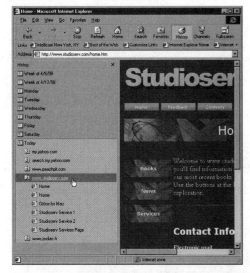

Figure 22. *Click the Web site folder to reveal the pages you visited at the site.*

Checking Your History

Checking your history allows you to view a list of the Web sites and Web pages you have visited recently. Remember: if you recall that you saw something interesting at a site recently, you can always check the history to see where you've been.

1. Click the History button on the toolbar to open the History Bar. **(Figure 21)**

2. Click a date or a week to open its entries.

3. Click a folder, which represents a Web site, to see a list of the pages on the site that you visited. **(Figure 22)**

4. Click a page to return to it.

✔ Tip

■ To see the address, and the date and time you last visited the page, click any link with the right mouse button and then choose Properties from the shortcut menu. **(Figure 23)**

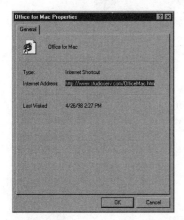

Figure 23. *Right-click a link and choose Properties.*

Checking Your History

Sending a Link to the Desktop

1. From the File menu, choose Send.

2. On the Send submenu, choose Shortcut to Desktop. **(Figures 24–25)**

✔ Tip

■ From the Desktop, you can drag the shortcut into a folder, into an e-mail message, or even onto the Links Bar in Internet Explorer.

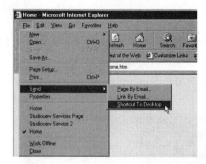

Figure 24. *Choose Shortcut to Desktop.*

Sending a Page or Link by E-Mail

To share something you've found on the Web, you can either send the Web Page or just a link to the page to someone else by e-mail.

1. From the File menu, choose Send.

2. On the Send submenu, choose Page by E-mail or Link by E-mail. **(Figure 26)**

Figure 25. *An Internet Explorer shortcut on the desktop.*

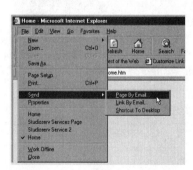

Figure 26. *Choose Page by E-mail or Link by E-mail.*

Sending a Link

Figure 27. *Click the Search button*

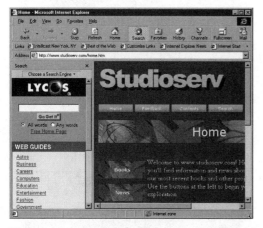

Figure 28. *Enter a search term and click Find.*

Figure 29. *The list of search engines.*

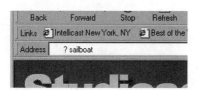

Figure 30. *Enter a quick search by entering a question mark followed by a search term.*

Searching the Web

1. Click the Search button on the toolbar. **(Figure 27)**

2. On the Search Bar at the left, enter a search term and click Find, Search, or Go Get It. **(Figure 28)**

✔ Tips

- The Search Bar always shows the search engine that is featured that day on the Microsoft Web site for Internet Explorer. To choose a different search engine, click the "Choose a Search Engine" link in the Search Bar. **(Figure 29)**

- You can perform a quick search by entering a question mark followed by a search term into the Address Bar. **(Figure 30)**

Searching the Web

Customizing the Links Bar

The Links Bar keeps a set of links handy on the screen. You can replace the standard links with your own favorite locations.

1. On the toolbar, click Favorites to open the Favorites Bar. **(Figure 31)**

2. Open the folder containing the favorite that you want.

3. Drag the favorite into position on the Links Bar. **(Figures 32–33)**

✔ **Tips**

■ You can also drag a link from any Web page onto the Links Bar.

■ To delete a link on the Links Bar, click it with the right mouse button and then choose Delete from the shortcut menu.

■ You can reposition links on the Links Bar by dragging them left or right.

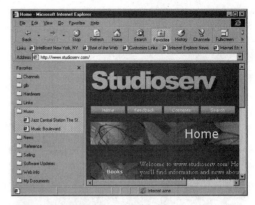

Figure 31. *Click Favorites to open the Favorites Bar.*

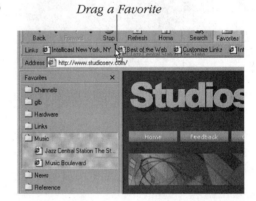

Figure 32. *Drag a Favorite to the Links Bar.*

Figure 33. *The new link.*

Customizing the Links Bar

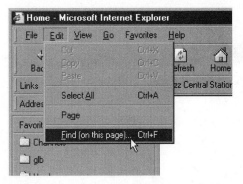

Figure 34. *Choose Find from the Edit menu.*

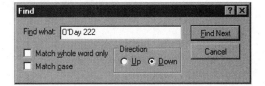

Figure 35. *Enter a Find term.*

Finding Text on a Web Page

After you've arrived at a Web page, you may want to find text quickly, especially if the page is long or if it contains a catalog listing.

1. From the Edit menu, choose Find. **(Figure 34)**
   or
   Press Ctrl+F.

2. Enter the text you want to find into the Find What field on the Find dialog box. **(Figure 35)**

3. Click Find Next. **(Figure 35)**

✔ Tip

■ By default, the Find program searches down the page, but if you are at the bottom of a lengthy page, you can change the Direction to Up on the Find dialog box and search up the page, instead.

Browsing Full Screen

To maximize the amount of screen space that Internet Explorer uses, you can switch to Full Screen view.

Click the Full Screen button on the toolbar. **(Figure 37)**

or

Press F11.

Full Screen button

Figure 36. *Click the Full Screen button.*

✔ Tips

■ To return to partial screen view, click the same button again.

■ While Internet Explorer is in Full Screen view, bump the mouse pointer against the bottom of the screen to bring up the Taskbar.

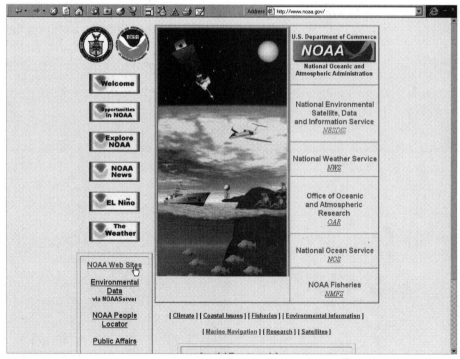

Figure 37. *Internet Exploirer full screen.*

Part 4
Portable and Workgroup Computing

Part 4
Portable and
Workgroup
Computing

Chapter 12: Portable Computing

Chapter 13: Connecting to a Network

Portable Computing

In This Chapter...

You will learn to take advantage of the many features in Windows 98 that are designed especially for people using portable computers.

In addition to the basic power management system that portable computers require to get the most out of their batteries, Windows also provides the Briefcase, a special folder on your portable computer to which you can copy files from a desktop computer. While you are traveling, you can work with the files in the Briefcase, and when you are reattached to the desktop computer, you can have the Briefcase synchronize the files between the desktop and the portable. Files in the Briefcase that are changed will be copied back to the desktop automatically.

Windows also provides several ways for you to connect a portable computer to a desktop. If the two computers are side by side, you can use a direct cable connection to link them. If the portable is on the road with you, you can use dial-up networking to connect your portable to the desktop back at home or back in the office.

About Portable Computing

For people who use portable computers for much, if not most, of their work, using Windows 98 will be a dream. Windows 98 makes it easy to connect to a desktop computer or office server and exchange files. The Briefcase, included with Windows 98, can handle the task of synchronizing files between your desktop computer and your portable. Windows will even recognize when you've docked your computer to a desktop docking station and change its settings accordingly.

Because many people who use portable computers also use PC Cards (formerly known as PCMCIA cards) to provide their machines with modems, network adapters, sound devices, and additional disk drives, Windows 98 provides full and easy-to-use support for PC Cards.

Finally, Windows 98 offers advanced power management that can work hand-in-hand with the power management built into your portable computer. You'll be able to keep an eye on the remaining capacity of your batteries by checking a special icon right on the Windows desktop.

✔ Tip

■ People who have limited disk space should install Windows 98 with the Portable installation option. This installs only the most essential Windows files and all of the services that are built in for portable computing.

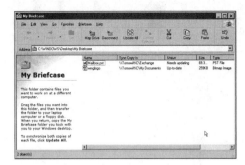

Figure 1. *The Briefcase.*

Figure 2. *The PC Card Properties dialog box.*

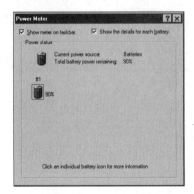

Figure 3. *The Power Meter dialog box.*

Figure 4. Click Listen to have your desktop computer (the host) wait for a portable computer to connect.

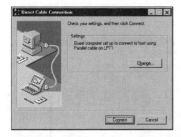

Figure 5. Click Connect to have your portable computer (the guest) connect to the host.

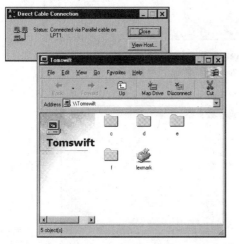

Figure 6. After the connection is established, the guest sees the host's shared resources.

Connecting to a Desktop with a Direct Cable Connection

A direct cable connection can simulate a true network connection.

1. Attach a cable between the serial or parallel ports of your desktop and portable computers.

2. On each computer, click the Start button and choose Programs from the Start menu. Then, on the Programs submenu, choose Accessories. On the Accessories submenu, choose Communications. Finally, on the Communications submenu, choose Direct Cable Connection.

3. On the desktop computer's Direct Cable Connection dialog box, you should see a Host "listening" on a parallel or serial cable. **(Figure 4)** On the portable, you should see a Guest "connecting." If not, click the Change button and then follow the steps of the Direct Cable Connection wizard. If the settings on the Direct Cable Connection dialog box are correct (Host listening, Guest connecting), and the proper cable type (serial or parallel), click the Connect button. **(Figure 5)**

4. After you see confirmation that the two computers have connected, a window on the portable will display the host's "shared" disks, folders, and printers. Copy files to and from the folders on the host as though you were copying files to and from folders on your portable's disk. **(Figure 6)**

5. To close the connection, click Close on the Direct Cable Connection dialog box on either machine.

Direct Cable Connection

Connecting to a Desktop with Dial-Up Networking

If you are traveling with your portable computer, you can call the desktop back at home or in your office with the portable's modem and connect over the phone line to simulate a network connection.

1. Double-click the My Computer icon.

2. In the My Computer window, double-click the Dial-Up Networking icon. **(Figure 7)**

3. In the Dial-Up Networking window, double-click the icon of the connection to your desktop computer. If you have not yet set up a connection icon, you must create a new connection by double-clicking the Make New Connection icon. **(Figure 8)**

4. In the Connect To dialog box, enter your password, if necessary, and then click Connect. **(Figure 9)**

5. After the computers connect, you will see a window on the portable which displays the "shared" folders on the desktop that you can access. Copy files to and from these folders as though you were copying them to and from folders on your portable's disk.

6. To disconnect, click the Disconnect button on the Dial-Up Networking dialog box.

Figure 7. *Double-click the Dial-Up Networking icon.*

Figure 8. *Double-click the connection to your desktop computer.*

Figure 9. *Click Connect to establish the connection.*

Dial-Up Networking

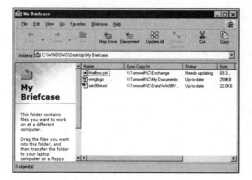

Figure 10. *The Briefcase.*

Figure 11. *The Briefcase confirms with you the files that need be updated.*

About the Briefcase

The Briefcase is a special program that keeps files in sync on both your desktop and portable computers. With the Briefcase, you don't have to track the changes you've made to files on both machines to be sure both machines have the latest copy of each file. The Briefcase can do the tracking for you, copying the latest version of each file to the other machine, if necessary.

To use the Briefcase, connect the two computers to the same network or connect them to each other by using a Direct Cable Connection or Dial-Up Networking.

Then, when the two computers are connected, copy the files you need from the desktop to the Briefcase on the portable. After you've modified the files on the portable, you can reconnect to the desktop later and tell the Briefcase to synchronize the files it holds. Any files that you have updated on the portable will replace the older versions on the desktop. Any files that you have updated on the desktop will replace the older versions on the portable. Any files that you have updated on both the desktop and the portable will not be changed on either machine.

About the Briefcase

Placing Files in the Briefcase

1. After you connect a portable and desktop computer, double-click the folder on the desktop computer that contains a file you want to place in the Briefcase. **(Figure 12)**

2. Drag the file icon to the My Briefcase icon on the portable computer's desktop. **(Figure 13)**

✔ Tips

■ To access a file that you've copied to the Briefcase, double-click the My Briefcase icon on the portable computer and then double-click the file you want. **(Figure 14)**

■ After you connect your desktop and portable computers, you may need to double-click Network Neighborhood on the portable computer to find the folder you want on the desktop computer.

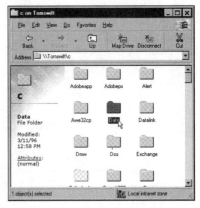

Figure 12. *From the portable computer, open the folder on the desktop that contains files you want to copy to the Briefcase.*

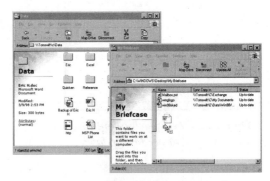

Figure 13. *From the portable computer, drag files from the desktop folder to the Briefcase.*

Figure 14. *Double-click a file in the Briefcase to open it.*

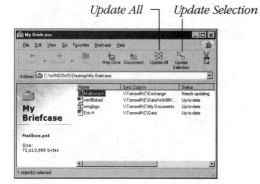

— *My Briefcase icon*

Figure 15. *Double-click the My Briefcase icon.*

Update All ⌐   Update Selection

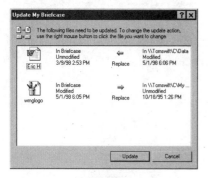

Figure 16. *Click Update All or Update Selection.*

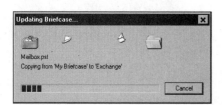

Figure 17. *Click Update.*

Figure 18. *The Updating Briefcase status box.*

Updating Files with the Briefcase

When you re-connect to the desktop computer, you can update the original files on the desktop with changes you've made to copies in the Briefcase on the portable.

1. Connect the desktop and portable computers by cable connection, network, or dial-up networking connection.

2. Double-click the My Briefcase icon on the portable computer. **(Figure 15)**

3. On the toolbar of the My Briefcase window, click the Update All button to perform all the updating.
   (Figure 16)

   or

   Select a single file to update and then click the Update Selection button.
   (Figure 16)

4. In the My Briefcase window, click Update to carry out the updates shown.   **(Figures 17–18)**

   or

   Click a file with the right mouse button if you want to change how the files shown will be updated.

✔ Tips

■ You can also choose Update All or Update Selection from the Briefcase menu.

■ A quick way to update all the files in the Briefcase is to click the My Briefcase icon with the right mouse button and then choose Update All from the shortcut menu.

■ To remove a file from the Briefcase, click the file and then press the Delete key.

Updating Files in the Briefcase

Using PC Cards (PCMCIA)

When you install Windows 98 on a portable computer with PC Card slots, the special software needed to use the slots will be installed on your machine automatically. When you insert a PC Card, Windows will recognize it immediately. If the appropriate software for the card is not installed, Windows will automatically install it.

To use a PC card, simply insert the card. An icon appears on the Taskbar. Before you remove a PC card, you should always stop the card by following these steps:

1. Double-click the PC Card icon on the Taskbar. **(Figure 19)**

2. On the PC Card (PCMCIA) Properties dialog box, select the PC card from the list. **(Figure 20)**

3. On the Properties dialog box, click Stop.

4. Click OK. Windows will tell you when it is safe to remove the PC card. **(Figure 21)**

✔ Tip

■ Windows signals with a double tone when it recognizes that a PC card has been inserted into a slot.

The PC Card icon.

Figure 19. *Double-click the PC Card icon.*

Figure 20. *Select the PC Card.*

Figure 21. *Click OK.*

Figure 22. *Double-click the Power Management icon.*

Suspending a Portable Computer

When Windows detects that your portable computer is running on its batteries, it can put the computer on standby after an interval of time that you can change.

1. In the Control Panel, double-click the Power Management icon. **(Figure 22)**

2. On the Power Scheme tab of the Power Management Properties dialog box, choose intervals after which the monitor and hard disks will be turned off. **(Figure 23)**

— *Change these intervals.*

Figure 23. *Change the "Turn off" intervals.*

Suspending a Portable Computer

Printing When You Are Away from Your Printer

With Windows 98, you can create print jobs even when your machine is not physically attached to a printer by working offline. Your print jobs will be held in the print queue. Then, when you return to the location of your printer, you can send all the print jobs from the print queue to the printer.

1. When disconnected from your printer, double-click the Printers icon in the My Computer window.

2. In the Printers window, click the icon of your printer with the right mouse button and choose Use Printer Offline from the shortcut menu. **(Figure 24)**

or

In the Printers window, double-click the icon for your printer and then choose Use Printer Offline from the Printer menu. **(Figure 25)**

3. When you re-connect to the printer, double-click the Printers icon in the My Computer window.

4. Double-click the icon of the printer.

5. From the Printers menu, choose Work Offline again. Your waiting print jobs will print to the printer.

✔ Tips

■ When a printer is set to work offline, its icon is grayed in the Printers window. **(Figure 26)**

■ When you return to your office, you can rearrange the order of print jobs by dragging documents up and down on the print queue list.

Figure 24. *Choose Use Printer Offline from the shortcut menu.*

Figure 25. *Choose Use Printer Offline from the printer dialog box.*

An offline printer is grayed out.

Figure 26. *A printer that is offline is grayed out.*

Printing When Away from the Printer

Figure 27. *Place the mouse pointer on the battery icon* without clicking.

Figure 28. *Double-click the battery icon to open the Power Meter dialog box.*

Checking the Battery Level

1. Place the mouse pointer on the battery icon on the Taskbar and pause without clicking. **(Figure 27)**

or

Double-click the battery icon to open the Power Meter dialog box. **(Figure 28)**

✔ Tip

■ To change the Power Meter settings, double-click the Power Management icon in the Control panel.

Docking and Undocking a Portable

If your portable has a docking station, you can connect the portable to the docking station and use your machine as if it was a desktop computer. Some portables allow "hot docking," or connecting while the portable is turned on. Check your machine's user manual to find out whether your machine has this capability.

Windows 98 maintains two hardware profiles for your portable computer and switches between them automatically when it detects that your computer has been docked or undocked. You can check these profiles on the Hardware Profiles tab of the System Properties dialog box.

1. Click My Computer with the right mouse button.

2. From the shortcut menu, choose Properties.

3. Click the Hardware Profiles tab on the System Properties dialog box. **(Figure 29)**

✔ **Tip**

■ To release your portable from its docking station, you should always choose the Eject PC command from the Start menu.

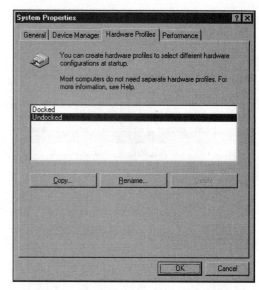

Figure 29. *The Hardware Profiles tab.*

Connecting to a Network

In This Chapter...

You will learn to use your computer on an office network, commonly called a LAN (Local Area Network).

A LAN allows the members of a work group to shared the resources of their computers. Members of the work group can swap files without having to copy them to diskettes, access programs on other computers, and print to printers that are on the network. This allows everyone to share resources. In fact, a resource such as a printer connected to your computer, or a folder on one of your disks that you want to make available to everyone else, is called "shared."

In this chapter, you will learn to browse other computers on the network, exchange files, print to network printers, and share the resources on your computer.

Browsing the Network

If your computer is connected to a network (also called a LAN), you may have access to shared resources on other computers in addition to those on your own computer system. For example, you may be able to open shared folders on other computers to which you've been given access, or you may be able to print to a shared printer that's attached to a computer somewhere else on the network. The Network Neighborhood icon makes it easy to find the shared resources that are available to you on your network.

1. On the Windows desktop, double-click the Network Neighborhood icon. **(Figure 1)**

2. In the Network Neighborhood window, double-click the icon of any of the shared computers or printers that you see. Only resources that are shared (made available to you) are visible in the window. **(Figure 2)**

   or

1. Click the Network Neighborhood icon with the right mouse button.

2. From the shortcut menu, choose Explore. **(Figure 3)**

3. Click a resource in the left pane to view its contents in the right pane of the Explorer. **(Figure 4)**

✔ Tip

■ In the Network Neighborhood window, you will see only other computers that are in your workgroup (a grouping of computers that can share resources).

Figure 1. *Double-click the Network Neighborhood icon.*

Figure 2. *Double-click a shared resource.*

Figure 3. *Choose Explore from the shortcut menu.*

Figure 4. *Click a resource in the left pane to see its contents in the right pane.*

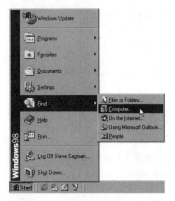

Figure 5. *Choose Computer from the Find submenu.*

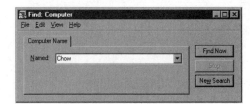

Figure 6. *Enter a computer name.*

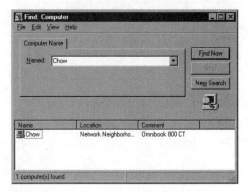

Figure 7. *Double-click a computer on the "found" list to view its shared resources.*

Finding a Computer

1. Click the Start button.
2. From the Start menu, choose Find.
3. From the Find submenu, choose Computer. **(Figure 5)**
4. In the Find: Computer dialog box, enter the computer name and then click Find Now. **(Figure 6)**
5. If the computer is found, it will be displayed in a list within the Find dialog box. You can double-click the computer name on this list to open the computer and view its shared folders. **(Figure 7)**

✔ Tip

■ You can also click the Network Neighborhood icon with the right mouse button and choose Find Computer from the shortcut menu.

Opening a Shared Folder on Another Computer

1. Double-click a computer shown in the Network Neighborhood window. **(Figure 8)**

2. In the next window that opens, double-click any shared folder. **(Figure 9)**

3. Double-click a file on a shared folder on another system.

or

1. Open a folder on your own computer and then, to move or copy files to and from a shared folder on another computer, drag and drop files between the windows for your computer and the shared folder on the other computer. **(Figure 10)**

✔ Tip

■ Depending on your access rights to the shared folder, you can either move, copy, and modify the files inside as though they were on your own system, or you can only read the files and not modify them.

Figure 8. *Double-click a computer in the Network Neighborhood window.*

Figure 9. *Double-click a shared folder.*

Figure 10. *You can drag and drop files between computers.*

Figure 11. *Double-click a computer that has a shared printer.*

Figure 12. *Double-click the printer icon.*

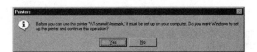

Figure 13. *Windows tells you that you need to set up the network printer on your computer.*

Printing to a Network Printer

1. In the Network Neighborhood window, double-click a computer that has a shared printer you want to use. **(Figure 11)**

2. Double-click the printer icon in the next window. **(Figure 12)** You may need to set up the printer before you can print. If so, Windows will guide you through the process. **(Figure 13)**

✔ Tip

■ After you access a shared printer on another computer, you can print to it as though it was a printer connected to your own computer.

Sharing a Folder or Printer

You can make the folders and printers that are part of your system available to other people on the network by sharing them.

1. Double-click the My Computer icon on the desktop.

2. Double-click a disk icon to see the folders you can share.

   or

   Double-click the Printers icon to see the printers you can share.

3. Click a folder, subfolder, or printer with the right mouse button and choose Sharing from the shortcut menu. **(Figure 14)**

4. In the Properties dialog box, click Shared As. **(Figure 15)**

5. Modify the Share Name if you want. **(Figure 16)**

6. For Access Type, choose Read-Only, Full, or Depends on Password. **(Figure 16)**

7. Enter the Read-Only, Full Access, or both Read-Only and Full Access passwords, depending on your choice in Step 6 and then click OK. **(Figure 16)**

✔ Tips

■ After you share a folder or printer, a cradling hand appears under the item's icon. **(Figure 17)**

■ In the Properties dialog box, you can change the share name to more fully describe the resource to other users.

■ To share resources on your computer, File and Print Sharing must be on. Double-click the Network icon in the Control Panel to change this setting.

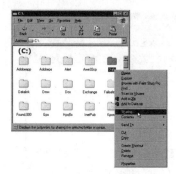

Figure 14. *Choose Sharing.*

Figure 15. *Click Shared As.*

Figure 16. *Enter the Share Name and Access info.*

Figure 17. *A shared resource icon.*

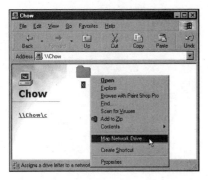

Figure 18. *Choose Map Network Drive.*

Figure 19. *Choose Reconnect at logon.*

Figure 20. *Mapped resources appear in My Computer*

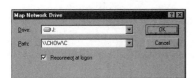

Figure 21. *Enter the name of the resource to map.*

Mapping a Network Drive

To make it easy to use the files in a shared folder on another computer, you can map the network drive to a drive letter on your system. For example, if your computer has a Drive C: and Drive D:, you can map a shared folder on another computer to Drive E:. The shared folder then appears in the My Computer window.

1. Double-click Network Neighborhood and then navigate to the shared folder to which you want to connect.

2. Click the shared folder with the right mouse button and choose Map Network Drive from the shortcut menu. **(Figure 18)**

3. In the Map Network Drive window, click Reconnect at Logon if you'll want to re-establish the connection automatically every time you log on to your computer. **(Figure 19)**

4. Click OK.

✔ Tips

■ Mapped resources appear as icons in the My Computer window. To open these folders, you can simply double-click their icons. **(Figure 21)**

■ If you know the name of the computer and shared folder to which you want to connect, you can click the My Computer or Network Neighborhood icons with the right mouse button, choose Map Network Drive, and then enter the path name into the Map Network Drive dialog box. The computer name is preceded by a double back slash, and the folder name is preceded by a single back slash. **(Figure 21)**

Index

Index

Index

Index